TWENTIETH
CENTURY
DANISH MUSIC

TWENTIETH CENTURY DANISH MUSIC

An Annotated Bibliography and Research Directory

Lansing D. McLoskey

Music Reference Collection, Number 65

GREENWOOD PRESS
Westport, Connecticut • London

Library of Congress Cataloging-in-Publication Data

McLoskey, Lansing D., 1964–
   Twentieth century Danish music : an annotated bibliography and
research directory / Lansing D. McLoskey.
     p. cm.—(Music reference collection, ISSN 0736–7740 ; no.
65)
   Includes bibliographical references and index.
   ISBN 0–313–30293–6 (alk. paper)
   1. Music—Denmark—20th century—Bibliography. 2. Music—
Denmark—20th century—Directories. I. Title. II. Series.
ML120.D3M35   1998
016.78′09489′0904—dc21   97–42760

British Library Cataloguing in Publication Data is available.

Library of Congress Catalog Card Number: 97–42760
ISBN: 0–313–30293–6
ISSN: 0736–7740

First published in 1998

Greenwood Press, 88 Post Road West, Westport, CT 06881
An imprint of Greenwood Publishing Group, Inc.

Printed in the United States of America

The paper used in this book complies with the
Permanent Paper Standard issued by the National
Information Standards Organization (Z39.48–1984).

10 9 8 7 6 5 4 3 2 1

Dedicated to Kyrie.

Contents

Preface

"Something is weird in the state of Denmark. The king rides a bicycle, and the density of musical composers per square kilometer exceeds that of all other countries."[1]

Something weird indeed. In a country of little more than five million people there is an inordinate amount of musical activity. Consider some of the statistics: ten symphony orchestras (not including numerous community orchestras and semi-professional orchestras), four opera companies, seven music conservatories, some fifteen classical music record labels, over a dozen classical music festivals, and an extraordinary number of composers.

Yet, for all the vitality in Danish musical life, Danish music remains in a state of relative obscurity outside of Scandinavia, even among those in the fields of composition and musicology. The majority of music history books and surveys of 20th century music ignore Denmark entirely. Those that do mention Denmark most often lump it together with Norway, Sweden and Finland in a brief chapter titled "Scandinavia," and then Carl Nielsen is often the only Dane named specifically.

The two most well known figures in Danish music history are certainly Dietrich Buxtehude (1637-1707) and Carl Nielsen (1865-1931), about whom numerous books, articles, and even films have been produced in recent years. There is a fair amount published about Danish music during the late 18th century and early 19th century (the "Danish Golden Age," when Friedrich Kuhlau resided and worked in Copenhagen), and in recent years much has been done in the field of Danish Renaissance music, in particular concerning the reign of Christian IV (r.1588-1648) during which time Heinrich Schütz and John Dowland worked in the Danish court.

This is not the case, however, when it comes to the 20th century. Until fairly recently there has existed somewhat of a rarefaction in research and publication outside of Denmark concerning Danish music, composers, theories and musical life following the death of Carl Nielsen. Anyone who has attempted in-depth research in the field is aware of this *lacuna* in scholarship and publication, and has doubtless become frustrated with the lack of any efficient way to find that information which does exist.

It was in this purpose that I undertook the task of compiling a comprehensive bibliography of printed matter in all languages. It became clear, however, that a mere bibliography would not suffice. Rather, what was needed was an annotated bibliography and research directory - not simply listing printed media, but also music organizations, public institutions, educational institutions, publishers, record companies, ensembles, etc.: a comprehensive map for people attempting to conduct research in the field or interested in programming Danish music. A resource such as this does not exist in any language, and the directories in Danish or other Scandinavian languages (such as *NOMUS-Katalogen* and *Dansk Musik Årbog*) are not comprehensive, nor do they include printed material or resources outside of Scandinavia.

DESCRIPTION OF CONTENTS

The work is divided into two parts, the Annotated Bibliography and the Research Directory, with each part divided into several sub-sections (refer to the table of contents). Citations in the bibliography are prefaced with a "B," those in the research directory with an "R."

Though the scope of the work encompasses all sources pertaining to Danish music, composers and musical life since 1900, the emphasis is on the post-Nielsen era (1931-present). Being that Carl Nielsen is such a familiar and prominent figure with a large and generally accessible body of work published about him, those sources focusing specifically on Nielsen are excluded.[2] The Faroe Islands are included, in view of their close affiliation with the Danish mainland. Greenland, the West Indies and other geographically and culturally remote former Danish colonies are not included.

The work attempts to be as comprehensive as possible, including publications in all languages and rare and out-of-print editions of historical significance. In cases where the author was not able to obtain access to a copy, sources are cited without annotation.

The bulk of printed material concerning 20th century Danish music is in the form of journals and periodicals published within Denmark and Scandinavia. By far the most important of these is *dmt* (*Dansk Musik-*

tidsskrift), a scholarly journal which since 1925 has covered all aspects of musical life in Denmark, including interviews with prominent musical figures and analyses of recent works. So numerous are the articles on Danish 20th century music in *dmt* that only a representational sample of important articles is included in this bibliography. Since 1980 *dmt* has published an annual index; for articles prior to 1980 it is indexed in *The Music Index* (1949-), RILM (1967-), and in *Bibliographie des Musikschrifttums* (1950-).

Until 1989 what few recordings of Danish music existed were produced primarily by Dansk Musik Antologi (The Danish Music Anthology), a private organization that worked in cooperation with EMI, Polydor/Phonogram, and Deutsche Grammophon to release Danish musical recordings. Following the passing of *Musikloven* (The Music Law) of 1989, Dansk Musik Antologi was replaced by the state-run organization Statslige Pladeselskab (The National Recording Society) and the newly formed dacapo label, with the sole purpose of recording and distributing Danish music on an international level. Subsequently, the amount of 20th century Danish music available on recordings has dramatically increased, and several foreign labels have taken an interest in Danish composers.

In an effort to accomplish this same end in the printed media, the journals *Musical Denmark* and *Nordic Sounds* are published in English by MIC (The Danish Music Information Centre). Unfortunately, neither are as scholarly as *dmt,* nor are they readily distributed in the United States. The result of this situation is that until quite recently it was necessary to be able to read Danish or another Scandinavian language in order to conduct substantial research on 20th century music in Denmark.

The last several years, however, have seen a dramatic rise in English and foreign language publications on the topic, as several Danish composers have received heightened international recognition and interest in Scandinavian music by scholars outside of Denmark has increased. This interest is reflected not only in publication, but also in research facilities outside of Denmark. In 1988 Ohio State University founded the Nordic Music Archive, containing the largest collection of music by Scandinavian composers in the United States, and 1996 saw the opening of two landmark research centers: The Japan Scandinavia Music Centre in Yamato-shi Kanagawa, Japan, and The Center for the Study of Danish Music at the University of Louisville, KY, the first research facility of its kind in the United States.

---

[1] Nicolas Slonimsky. *Baker's Biographical Dictionary of Musicians.* 8th ed. (New York: Schirmer Books, 1992), 157.

    [2] A thorough annotated bibliography and research guide focusing on Carl Nielsen exists in the form of Mina F. Miller's *Carl Nielsen: A Guide to Research* (New York: Garland Publishing, Inc., 1987). A bibliography listing publications issued in the interim can be found in *The Nielsen Companion*, Ed. Mina F. Miller (Portland, OR: Amadeus Press, 1994).

Twentieth Century Danish Music: A Brief Overview

The composer Rued Langgaard (1893-1952) had a difficult life, a fact he was not hesitant to share with the world. An eccentric and paradoxical figure, he was a staunch anti-modernist while at the same time composing music that only in recent years has been recognized as being decades ahead of its time. A prolific composer, he composed some of the most original and prophetic works in the history of Nordic music, such as the massive *Sfærerenes Musik* (*Music of the Spheres*, 1918). Nonetheless, he was never accepted by the Danish musical establishment and spent the majority of his lifetime as a bitter yet prolific outsider.

In 1948 Langgaard composed a work titled *Carl Nielsen, vor store Komponist* (*Carl Nielsen, Our Great Composer*). Scored for large symphony orchestra and chorus, the performance indication on the score is "with all one's might." The entire work is only thirty-two measures long and is constructed in such a way that the ending wraps around to the beginning, which the composer then instructs "to be repeated for all eternity." And the text? Nothing but the words "Carl Nielsen, our great composer," over and over again.

What is the significance of this story? Is this simply a case of symphonic-sour-grapes by a Danish Salieri-figure? Yes and no. Langgaard wrote the piece not as a serious work but rather as a scathing, sarcastic attack on the musical establishment which he submitted on more than one occasion to the Danish National Radio. Yet below the surface of the story lies a poignant statement concerning the musical milieu and attitudes concerning Danish music in the first half of this century, both in and outside of Denmark; conditions which are pertinent - if not largely responsible - for the current situation concerning publications and international awareness of Danish music.

For much of the history of Western music, Denmark has been viewed as a provincial backwater. When compared to its European counter- parts, Denmark, not unlike other countries peripheral to the mainstream of continental music represented especially by the Italian and Austro-Germanic traditions, usually lagged years behind the musical developments of its more sophisticated neighbors.

The majority of the well known composers who worked in Denmark were, in fact, not Danish: Dowland was of course English, Schütz and Kuhlau were German, and though Buxtehude's birth heritage was Danish he spent his adult life in Lübeck, Germany, and as a composer is associated with the Northern German school. The relatively few native composers most often studied abroad and upon returning home were content to write in a derivative style. Additionally, it is relevant to note that the music emulated by Danish composers from the Renaissance through the 19th century was almost exclusively the conservative rather than the innovative: Palestrina rather than Marenzio; Brahms and Mendelssohn rather than Wagner, Strauss or Mahler.[1, 2]

It was not until the so-called "Danish Golden Age" which coincided with the rise of musical nationalism across Europe, that Denmark began to have a thriving musical life of its own with native composers incorporating Danish folk tunes in their music. However, even the most successful of these composers - such as Niels W. Gade (1817-1890), J.P.E. Hartmann (1805-1900) and Hans Christian Lumbye (1810-1874) - had relatively limited international recognition compared to their continental counterparts, and musical trends and aesthetic tastes within Denmark generally followed the mainstream continental developments, especially those from Germany.

During the first two decades of the 20th century when the European musical scene was bursting at the seams with numerous new and revolutionary developments, Denmark was busily engaged in an endeavor of its own: self definition. These years saw the emergence of a strong, central musical figure appropriately and literally from the roots of Danish peasants. This was the era of Carl Nielsen, who from 1900 until his death in 1931 came to be practically synonymous with Danish music. As composer, director of the Royal Opera, conductor of the symphony, director and then chair of the Royal Danish Conservatory of Music, writer, teacher, and chairman of the powerful Music Society his influence - both direct and indirect - was to shape the face of Danish musical life and establishment for decades. Those who dissented from his views found themselves as outsiders with little hope for recognition, within or outside of Denmark. Just as Grieg became synonymous with Norwegian music and Sibelius with Finnish, the world considered Nielsen to be the one Danish name to remember, to the point of exclusion.

What exactly was the Nielsen sound, and why did it resonate so strongly with the Danish audience? It has been said that the "Danishness" of Nielsen is not easy to define, but it is nevertheless something which any Dane can (or claims to) hear. This illusive quality may have something to do with the infusion of the "colour of folklore in the fabric of his musical language, a colouring of something familiar and reassuring even at his most daring and experimental."[3]

A steadfast believer in traditional values amid experimentation, Nielsen was nonetheless a committed "modernist." The modernism of Nielsen, however, is not to be confused with that of his contemporaries Schoenberg or Stravinsky. His was not a modernism of tortured chromaticism, violent juxtapositions or emotional angst. Philosophically he was much closer to the modernism of Bartôk, though only remotely so in terms of æsthetics and technique. He was not so much interested in destroying tonality or even pushing it to its limits, but rather in exploring the edges of tonality and molding it into a plastic, flexible entity. All the while Nielsen kept a certain humor and self-irony even in his serious works - an important aspect of his music which rings home with the Danish people who have an affinity for the merrier side of life. Though the prevailing mood of much of his work is melancholic, a certain lightheartedness is sparkling just beneath the surface as an "ever present counterpoint to symphonic grandeur and romantic seriousness."[4]

Of course there were casualties. Most composers found themselves under the overwhelming shadow of Nielsen and willingly submitted to his musical ideas. However, the Nielsen heritage "proved easy to administer only for the lesser spirits, and became a veritable hindrance to the greater ones."[5] There was little tolerance for non-conformers such as Langgaard.

The years following Nielsen's death did see a gradual exploration of some imported developments, beginning with Jean Sibelius. In the Finnish master was found a companion spirit to Nielsen, if not in actual technique or language in a kindred "Nordic lyricism." His late-tonal style, along with that of Nielsen, represented the unofficial norm for all composers to follow at the time, and composers of the next several generations were likewise strongly influenced by the two.

This is not to say that continental developments were entirely without influence. In typical fashion, however, those ideas stemming from below the border which were most influential were not the extreme or revolutionary, but rather the more refined and subdued: i.e., impressionism and neo-classicism rather than expressionism and serialism. Prominent composers in the years following Nielsen's death were Knudåge Riisager (1897-1974), Finn Høffding (b.1899-1997), Jørgen Jersild (1913-1993), Herman D. Koppel (b.1908), and Niels Viggo Bentzon (b.1919). Høffding and Jersild were influenced by French impressionism while continuing to write music that was nevertheless permeated by an indefinable Nordic character. Riisager and Koppel, on the other hand, were influenced by the neo-classicism of Stravinsky and Hindemith. Gunnar Berg (1909-89), the only composer to embrace Schoenberg's twelve-tone system, suffered much the same fate as Langgaard before him, struggling in poverty for most of his career.

In addition to being a virtuosic pianist and one of the most notable composers of his generation, Niels Viggo Bentzon holds the distinction of being the most prolific Danish composer of the entire 20th century. In describing the composer, Nicolas Slonimsky comments that "the sheer quantity of his works precludes total enumeration lest it burst open the very limit of the present edition."[6] His list of opus numbers exceeds 630, and he continues to be active as a composer, performer and writer to this day. Though his early works were neo-classical in style, he soon began to incorporate a wide variety of ultra-modern techniques, including serialism, happenings, graphic notation, multi-media forces, performance-art and aleatorism in every genre of concert music, opera, and dance.

The preeminent figure of the post-Nielsen period was Vagn Holmboe (1909-96), who combined an unusual interest in folk music of the Baltic region with a personal extension of Brahmsian developing-variation into what he called "Metamorphosis technique." Arguably the most influential teacher after Carl Nielsen, a list of his students is a virtual who's-who of Danish contemporary music. Like Nielsen, he preferred to explore the edges of tonality rather than pursue what he perceived as unnecessary revolutions of the Second Viennese composers or Stravinsky. In 1933 Holmboe concisely expressed the then prevalent view among Danish composers:

> Are there not three main threads from Romanticism down to the music of today? The first thread leads through Wagner-Strauss down to Schoenberg. The other from Chopin through Debussy down to Stravinsky. Finally, the third thread goes from Brahms to Carl Nielsen and Bartôk ... *The question of in which thread we find health, strength and positive content is surely not open to discussion.*[7] (italics added)

This identification of a specific neo-tonal style with national identity was accepted by many in the musical establishment, including a young talent named Per Nørgård (b.1932). In several of his early writings Nørgård warned against any return to central European music for inspiration as Denmark had for so many centuries, urging instead a focus on the strength and individuality he believed to be inherent in "the universe of the Nordic mind."

> It is as if in order to find a stronger consciousness about ourselves and our own natural traits we become passive and 'eclectic-ized,' always considering what is being done to the south ... Isn't it about time that we dare to put more confidence in the wide, Nordic basis? Is the musical situation south and east of us really so blooming and seductively fertile that we absolutely must consider it before ourselves?[8]

In part this attitude reflected the horror felt by the Danish people in the aftermath of the Nazi atrocities and the devastation of World War II, which had a profoundly negative effect on attitudes toward all aspects of German culture. Danish artists - as the rest of the citizenry - retreated somewhat and found safety in cool, rational objectivity. The eminent Danish musicologist Jørgen I. Jensen writes:

> As is known, in Germany we saw a culture or mentality where it seemed that an entire people had been gripped by irrational feeling. So it is no wonder that objectivity became the refuge. Obviously, the majority of Danish composers between 1930 and 1960 had to struggle to turn their music in a direction other than German. Of course, there was a strong influence from Hindemith, but that was as a neo-objective functionalist rather than a 'German' composer. Otherwise, one turned towards the East, (which had) a kind of connection to the Nordic use of modal movements ... which goes all the way back to Carl Nielsen ... Other composers turned towards France.[9]

Atonal expressionism and twelve-tone music were perceived as symptoms of the German irrationalism that led to Nazism, totalitarianism, and the barbarism of the War. Skepticism of anything too "emotionally-Germanic" can be heard in both the music and writings of Danish composers. For example, though Niels Viggo Bentzon was the first to lecture and write on Schoenberg in Denmark,[10] one can nevertheless detect an echo of the previously quoted Holmboe statement in his words: "... he (Schoenberg) is the child of Tristanian decadence; romanticism's sick twin brother, with Brahms the healthy twin."[11]

Yet, was not Brahms German? Yes, but as Hindemith he represented to the Danes the rational, non-threatening side of German culture, not the "sick," untrustworthy side found in Wagner, Strauss, Schoenberg and the Second Viennese School. It is ironic that despite the fact that Schoenberg was reviled by the Nazis, he nonetheless symbolized the turbulent, obsessive "emotional tyranny" which was perceived by the Danes as impending cultural imperialism. Such attitudes persisted into the 1970's in Denmark, and resentment of Germany's continuing predominance in international musical life still smolders.

It is paradoxical that the event that crucially changed the course of Danish music was, in fact, a direct result of contact with the continental (and German!) avant-garde. In 1960 three of the most important composers of the youngest generation, Per Nørgård, Ib Nørholm (b.1931) and Pelle Gudmundsen-Holmgreen (b.1932), attended the ISCM Festival at Cologne, where they heard works by Ligeti, Boulez and Stockhausen. Neither they nor Danish musical life would ever be the same. The waters of the European avant-garde with all its new ideas and possibilities were rising, and these three volunteered to open the floodgates wide.

In typical Danish fashion the various compositional possibilities were not taken at face value or embraced dogmatically. Serial music now represented only one challenge among many, and as such was less threatening and more inviting for exploration. Rather than developing into a full-fledged school, however, these experimentations were quickly followed by music collage, concretism, and aleatoric music as "parallel developments."[12] Nørgård, Nørholm and Gudmundsen-Holmgreen immediately embarked upon three very distinct and individual paths and were instrumental in the conversion of their peers, as well as composers of the older generation.

Nørgård was already the most important figure of the young generation. After the revelatory ISCM Festival he began a series of brief experimentations with serialism and graphic notation. Quickly realizing both the potential within *and* simultaneous claustrophobic systematics inherent to twelve-tone music and the ultra-serialism of Boulez, he started exploring other aspects of serial technique. This lead eventually to his "infinity row" theory (having ultimately little in common with mainstream serialism), which in turn lead to his theory of "Hierarchic music," a sort of complex heterophony. Since then he has developed several unique theories (such as "tone seas," astrological/mystical relationships, and combinatorial tones), and has worked extensively with the work of the schizophrenic Swiss artist Adolf Wölfi (1864-1930).

After brief forays into serialism, Nørholm and Gudmundsen-Holmgreen began a movement called Ny Enkelhed (New Simplicity). The simplicity in each of their musics, however, was of an entirely different nature, so that despite the fact that they were aligned with the same movement their paths were unique.

Gudmundsen-Holmgreen's music became so simple that, in the composer's own words, the music is "poor in material, non-dramatic, without pathos, without expansion and culmination ... boring for the listener ... [and] immensely boring to play."[13] While this is perhaps a tongue-in-cheek exaggeration, he has indeed pushed simplicity to its extremes. In later years he has juxtaposed simple surfaces with complex forms, developing a sort of expressionistic-minimalism.

Nørholm's simplicity, on the other hand, was one of simple lines and textures. His music owes much more to the Nordic æsthetic of Holmboe, Sibelius and Nielsen, yet boiled down to its lyric essence. Composers who later identified themselves with New Simplicity, such as Ole Buck (b.1945) and Hans Abrahamsen (b.1952), write music equally disparate.

Nørholm and several others also pursued the idea of stylistic plurality *within* a single musical work. Thus, within a multi-movement work may be found free-atonality, graphic notation, Hindemith-style tonal sections and a twelve-tone finale. A comparison may be made with the pastiches of post-modernism, a main difference being that the pluralism here is a collage of modern composition techniques rather than quotations of past eras.

Technology in music came somewhat slowly to Denmark. Early pioneers in the field of electronic and tape music were Jørgen Plætner (b.1930) and Else Marie Pade (b.1924), who is also notable as being one of the first woman composers in the world to work in the field of electronic music. Today Denmark boasts state-of-the-art electro-acoustic and computer-music facilities, lead by composers such as Ivar Frounberg (b.1950) and American emigrant Wayne Siegel (b.1953).

In recent years Poul Ruders (b.1949) has emerged as one of the most distinctive voices in European music and currently has the largest international following of any Dane. Largely a self-taught composer, his music is unique yet nonetheless highly crafted. Early works were influenced by mediæval, Renaissance and Baroque music; as a result he was frequently labeled a "post-modernist." During the past decade, however, his music has become increasingly dramatic and gestured to the point of extremism. He is eager to push music to its absolute limits in all directions - simplicity, virtuosity, repetition, tempo, register, or sheer volume - and his music has a bombastic-yet-spiritual quality not unlike that of Messian. In a much-quoted phrase, Ruders describes himself as a "film composer with no film." The film conjured up by his music, however, is a collage of non-sequiturs, dream sequences, religious visions, and ultra-violence, closer to *A Clockwork Orange* than to *The Sound of Music.*

Composers of the generations following Nørgård, Nørholm and Gudmundsen-Holmgreen have been raised in a time and environment where "pluralism is a given."[14] Figures such as Niels la Cour (b.1944), Bo Holten (b.1948), Bent Lorentzen (b.1935) and Karl Aage Rasmussen (b.1947) have pursued completely individual paths, and it would be difficult, if not impossible, to categorize them as members of any movement or school. Similarly, those of the younger generation such as Mogens Christensen (b.1955) and Bent Sørensen (b.1958) have been reluctant to embrace any one given style, giving contemporary Danish music a profile that is both vibrant and constantly in flux.

Though diversity is indeed a trademark of our century, for Denmark it has become a flag around which to rally. Denmark has broken free from the bonds of self-imposed stylistic unity as well as submission (and the corresponding paranoia of submission) to foreign musical trends. The very concept of "style" is being challenged, and new definitions are being proposed. In a time when national styles have essentially vanished, it is entirely appropriate that the individuality of Danish music among the music of the world be simply the individuality of individual Danish composers.

---

[1] Though the Danes Mogens Pedersøn (c.1580-1623) and Melchior Borchgrevinck (d.1632) both studied with Giovanni Gabrieli in Venice, neither of their music is nearly as progressive or innovative as that of their distinguished teacher.

[2] "... there is no way around the fact that one of the more telling dates in Danish musical life is the year of the first Danish performance of Gustav Mahler's *Sixth Symphony* - (not until) 1970 ..."   Jørgen I. Jensen. "A Sense of Form and Clandestine Meetings with Expressionism." *Nordiska Musikfester/ Nordic Music Days: 100 Years.* Sten Hanson, ed. (Stockholm: Kunglige Musikaliska akademien, 1988), 12.

[3] Karl Aage Rasmussen. *Noteworthy Danes: Portraits of Eleven Danish Composers.* (Copenhagen: Edition Wilhelm Hansen), 10.

[4] Ibid., 10.

[5] Ibid., 11.

[6] Nicolas Slonimsky. "Bentzon, Niels Viggo." *Baker's Biographical Dictionary of Musicians.* 8th ed. (New York: Schirmer Books, 1992), 157.

[7] Jensen. "A Sense of Form ...", 13-14.

[8] Per Nørgård. "Samarbejde - samfølelse." *Nordisk Musikkulter.* 3 (1956): 66. Trans. Lansing D. McLoskey.

[9] Jensen. "A Sense of Form ...", 13.

[10] Among other things, Bentzon wrote the first book published in Denmark on twelve-tone composition: *Tolvtoneteknik* (Copenhagen: Wilhelm Hansen, 1953). Though noteworthy for its position in Danish music history, the work nevertheless reveals a fundamental lack of understanding about Schoenberg's theories as well as his application of twelve-tone technique.

[11] Jensen. "A Sense of Form ...", 14.

[12] Ibid., 17.

[13] Rasmussen. *Noteworthy Danes*, 52.

[14] Jørgen I. Jensen. "Tide og utide: Omkring Karl Aage Rasmussens tids-symfoni." *dmt.* 5/6 (1984/85), 263.

Guidelines and Abbreviations

Unless otherwise indicated, all sources are in the same language as their title.

Entries are listed alphabetically following Danish grammatical rules; i.e. the Danish vowels æ, ø and å follow z. This is contrasted with vowels with *umlautes* (ä, ö and ü), where the *umlautes* do not affect alphabetization. Some Danish words - especially proper names - may be spelled interchangeably with either an å or two adjacent a's (such as "Århus" and "Aarhus," "Nørgård" and "Nørgaard"); this is most common in sources written prior to c. 1950. In these cases, entries are alphabetized according to the spelling as it appears in the actual source.

Likewise, publisher names are cited as they appear in the source. For example, in an English publication the name of the publisher may be given in an English translation. Citations are in strict MLA format.

COMMON ABBREVIATIONS:

DIEM	Danish Institute of Electroacoustic Music
dmt	*Dansk Musiktidskrift*
MIC	Dansk Musik Informations Center (Danish Music Information Centre)
nd.	"No date given"
np.	"No publisher given", "no place given" or "no page given," depending on the context within the citiation.

Acknowledgments

First and foremost, I would like to express my utmost gratitude to Bendt Viinholt Nielsen, Kim Bonfils and Svend Ravnkilde at The Danish Music Information Centre for their invaluable assistance, without which this book would not have been possible. Additional thanks go to Edition Wilhelm Hansen, The Nordic Music Archive, and the numerous people at libraries, publishers and institutions here and in Denmark who contributed to this project over the past four years. Lastly, I thank my wife Kathleen for her untiring patience and steadfast support.

BIBLIOGRAPHY

Books and Reference Sources

B1.   Albeck, Gustav, ed. *Vort første by- og landsdelsorkester: Aarhus By-orkester, 1935-1960.* Aarhus: Universitetsforlaget, 1960. 112 p.

A history of the Aarhus community orchestra in commemoration of its 25th anniversary. Includes list of works performed.

B2.   Alsinger, Bent Friis. *Komponisten Svend S. Schultz - et kapitel af dansk musikliv.* Karlslunde: Friis musiskforlag, 1996. 72 p.

Informative biography of the composer Svend Schultz, with contributions by friends, family and colleagues. Includes selective list of important works.

B3.   Andersen, Mogens, and Niels Bo Foltmann, Claus Røllum-Larsen, eds. *Festskrift Jan Maegaard.* Copenhagen: Engstrøm & Sødring, 1996. 348 p.

Festchrift honoring the 70th birthday of the eminent Danish composer/musicologist Jan Maegaard. Divided into three main sections: Schoenberg studies (a specialty of Maegaard's), Music Theory, and Danish Musical Life in the 20th century. Of special interest are an article by Dan Fog on musical events and developments in Denmark from 1919-1926, Søren Sørensen's article on the Danish composer/musicologist Knud Jeppesen, and an overview of Maegaard's compositional activites by Erling Kullberg with a complete work list and discography. Also includes five short "musical greetings" by Axel Borup-Jorgensen, Peter Brask, Tage Nielsen, Niels Rosing-Schow and Karlheinz Stockhausen.

B4.   Ardley, Neil and Poul Ruders. *A Young Person's Guide to Music.*
       London: Dorling Kindersley Books, 1995. 80 p.

       To celebrate the 300th anniversary of the death of Purcell and the
       50th anniversary of Britten's *The Young Person's Guide to the
       Orchestra*, the BBC commissioned Poul Ruders to write a similar
       work, titled *Concerto in Pieces.* Aimed primarily at children, the
       book discusses the orchestra in general using the *Concerto in Pieces*
       for numerous examples and includes a CD of the work.

B5.   Bech, Svend Cedergreen, ed. *Dansk biografisk leksikon.* 3rd
       edition. 16 vols. + supplement (26 p.). Copenhagen: Gyldendal,
       1979-1995.

       Continuance of the *Dansk biografisk leksikon* series (*see* B23).
       Strongest for popular culture and political figures, though includes
       many prominent Danish composers, conductors and musicians.
       Photos, bibliographical references and indexes.

B6.   Bengtsson, Ingmar, ed. *Modern Nordisk Musik; Fjorton tonsättare
       om egna verk.* Stockholm: Natur och Kultur, 1957. 260 p.

       Essays from fourteen composers from Denmark, Norway and
       Sweden discussing their own works. Includes discussions of
       "metamorphosis" technique by Vagn Holmboe and Niels Viggo
       Bentzon as found in their 7th and 4th symphonies, respectively, and
       an analysis of *Davids-salme* by Herman D. Koppel. Numerous
       musical examples. Selective work lists.

B7.   Bengtsson, Ingmar. *Musikvidenskab--nu og i fremtiden.*
       Copenhagen: Folkeuniversitetet i København, 1978. 31 p.

B8.   Bengtsson, Ingmar. "The Symphony Worldwide: Scandinavia."
       The Symphony. Ed. Ursula von Rauchhaupt. London: Thames and
       Hudson, 1973. 247-56.

B9.   Behrendt, Flemming. *Fra et hjem med klaver: Herman D. Koppels
       liv og erindringer.* Copenhagen: H. Reitzel, 1988. 202 p.

       Biography of the composer. Includes indexes, bibliography, and list
       of works.

B10. Beyer, Anders, ed. *The Music of Per Nørgård. Fourteen Interpretive Essays.* London: Scolar Press, 1996. 304 p. Excellent collection of essays on the life, theories, impact and music of Per Nørgård. Valuable as both an introduction to and overview of Nørgård's work for those new to the subject, as well as to those familiar with his music. It is of particular significance being the first major reference source on Nørgård in English. Contributions by several prominent Danish musicologists and composers as well as one by Jean Christensen, an American musicologist specializing in the music of Nørgård. Includes a full-length CD with numerous musical examples, selective list of works and discography.

B11. Bonde, Lars Ole, ed. *Fra Århusopera til Landsopera. Den jyske Opera gennem 50 år 1947-97.* Aarhus: Den jyske Opera, 1997. 318 p.

B12. Bonde, Lars Ole, ed. *Randers Byorkester gennem 50 år.* Randers, Denmark: Randers Byorkester, 1995. 96 p.

Written in commemoration of the 50th anniversary of the Randers City Orchestra, divided into four chapters on the history, conductors, and "orchestral musical life" of the orchestra. Includes a register of repertoire, musicians, recordings, premieres and soloists.

B13. Bruun, Kai Aage. *Dansk Musiks Historie fra Holberg-tiden til Carl Nielsen.* 2 vols. Copenhagen: Vinten, 1969.

As the title suggests, the focus is on the eras prior and up to Carl Nielsen; nevertheless provides a good background and context to the early years of the twentieth century. 2nd volume focuses on the late 19th and early 20th centuries.

B14. Carlsson, Anders and Jan Ling, eds. *Nordisk musik och musikvetenskap under 1970-talet : en rapport fran 8:e Nordiska musikforskarkongressen, Ljungskile folkhogskola 25-30 juni 1979.* Göteborg: Musikvetenskapliga institutionen, Goteborgs universitet, 1980. 334 p.

Report from the 8th Nordic Musicology Convention in 1979. Illustrations, musical examples. Some coverage of contemporary Danish music.

B15.   Christensen, Erik. *The Musical Timespace* 2 vols. Ålborg: Ålborg Universitetsforlag, 1996. 264 p.

A "theory of the musical dimensions in time and space that call forth the experience of music." Includes numerous musical examples, appendix with extensive musical excerpts and analysis of several works. Though not specifically about Danish music it does include references to several Danish works and composers, including Per Nørgård and Rued Langgaard, among others.

B16.   Christensen, Jean. "Dansk Musik Tidsskrift." *International Music Journals.* Eds. Linda M. Fidler and Richard S. James. Westport, CT: Greenwood Press, 1990. 111-114.

Description of the contents, format, history, and publishing information for *dmt.*

B17.   Chopard, Patrice. *Ib Nørholm. Tradition in seiner Musik und seinem Denken: Analyse seiner 9. Symphonie.* Hamburg: Universität Hamburg, 1996. 137 p.

Thorough analysis of Nørholm's *9th Symphony.* Musical examples.

B18.   *Dansk Musikforskning frem mod år 2000. Rapport fra seminar den 11. maj 1994.* Copenhagen: Statens Humanistiske Forskningsråd, 1996. 102 p.

Report from the seminar on musicology held by the National Council for Humanities Studies held in 1994. Includes article by Finn Egeland Hansen on musicology and technology.

B19.   Dibelius, Ulrich. *Moderne Musik II: 1965-1985.* Munich: R. Piper GmbbH & Co., 1988.

Contains very brief summary of contemporary Danish music, briefly mentioning Per Nørgård, Ib Norholm and Pelle Gudmundsen-Holmgreen.

B20.   Dyssegaard, Søren. *The Royal Danish Ballet.* Copenhagen: Udenrigsministeriets Presse- og Informationsafdeling, 1969. 48 p.

B21.   Egeland Hansen, Finn. "Den rene stemning i renaissancetiden og hos Per Nørgård." *Festskrift til Otto Mortensen på 70-årsdagen den 18.*

*august 1977: fra kolleger og tidligere studerende ved Musik-
videnskabeligt Institut, Aarhus Universitet.* Aarhus: Publimus, 1977.

Interesting essay on voice leading in the Renaissance and the music
of Per Nørgård. Musical examples.

B22.   Eilskov, Tine and Kirsten Hede Jensen. *Musikinformation - en
vejviser et center: Dansk Musik Informations Center.* Copenhagen:
Danmarks Biblioteksskole, 1984. 236 p.

"Surveys the history and activity of the Danish Music Information
Center (MIC), focusing on the coverage by the media prior to its
public opening. Provides a directory of Danish institutions that are
relevant for information retrieval in music ... and gives details about
available materials and services."[1]

B23.   Engelstoft, Povl and Svend Dahl, eds. *Dansk biografisk leksikon.*
27 vols. Copenhagen: J. H. Schultz forlag, 1933-44.

A multi-volume biographical dictionary of important Danish figures
from all aspects of society, started in 1887 by Carl Frederik Bricka.
Includes bios of many of the prominent Danish composers,
conductors and musicians active during the period, though intended
for a non-scholarly audience. Bibliographical references and
indexes. Selected work lists for composers. *See also* B5.

B24.   *Festskrift til Otto Mortensen på 70-årsdagen den 18. august 1977:
fra kolleger og tidligere studerende ved Musik-videnskabeligt
Institut, Aarhus Universitet.* Aarhus: Publimus, 1977. 140 p.

Festschrift for composer/musicologist Otto Mortensen. Includes
several articles on 20th century Danish music. Bibliographic
references.

B25.   Finney, Ian. *The String Quartets of Vagn Holmboe.* Ph.D.
dissertation, University of London, Royal Holloway and Bedford
New College. London: University of London, 1988.

B26.   Ford, Andrew. *Composer to composer: Conversations about
contemporary music.* London: Quartet Books, Ltd., 1993. 252 p.

Compilation of interviews with 30 composers active in the last half
of the 20th century. Includes interview with Poul Ruders. Photos.

B27.   Frank, Tine. *Rued Langgaards Symfonier 6 -16: En analyse af forholdet mellem den symfoniske stil og det religiøst-symbolistiske indhold.* Cand. Mag. thesis. Copenhagen: Musikvidenskabeligt Institut, 1993. 107 p.

An "analysis of the relation between symphonic style and religious-symbolic content" in the symphonies of Langgaard. Explores his attitudes and beliefs about art, life, spirituality and the role of the artist, with an emphasis on the connection of late Romantic symbolism in literature and painting. Analyses, musical examples, extensive bibliography.

B28.   Friis, Niels. *Det Kongelige Kapel: fem aarhundreder ved hoffet, paa teatret og koncertsalen.* Copenhagen: P. Haase & Søns forlag, 1948. 350 p.

A history of the Royal Danish Orchestra published in commemoration of its 500th anniversary. Of particular interest is the final chapter ("De sidste aar") which discusses the years 1930-1948.

B29.   Glahn, Henrik, ed. *Dansk Musik.* Copenhagen: np., 1968.

B30.   Gram, Peder. *Moderne Musik.* Copenhagen: Udvalget for Folkeoplysnings Fremme, 1934. 165 p.

B31.   Grøndahl, Marianne. *Positioner: den Kongelige Danske ballet 1980-1994.* Copenhagen: Gyldendal, 1994. 143 p.

B32.   Hamburger, Povl, ed. *Aschehougs musikleksikon.* Copenhagen: Aschehoug, 1957-1958.

"An encyclopedia of terms, topics and biographies that is of particular interest for its personal name entries. International coverage, but strongest for Scandinavians."[2]

B33.   Hamburger, Povl. *Thomas Laub. Hans Liv og Gerning.* Copenhagen: Aschehoug, 1957. 160 p.

B34.   Hansen, Finn Egeland. *En oversigt over de vigtigste europæiski tone artsystemer fra antikken til vore dage og en kritisk redegørelse for deres akustiski og æstetiske teorier.* Unpublished thesis. 1963.

B35.   Hansen Finn Egeland, and Arthur Ilfeldt, Steen Pade, Christian Thodberg, eds. *Festskrift Søren Sørensen.* Copenhagen: Dan Fog,

1990. 310 p.

Festschrift for the Danish musicologist Søren Sørensen. Several articles on contemporary Danish composers and musical life, and contributions by composers. In Danish, English, German, and Swedish. Includes bibliographical references.

B36.   Hansen, Ivan, ed. *Per Nørgård; artikler 1962-1982*. Copenhagen: Ivan Hansen, 1982. 326 p.

An excellent survey of Per Nørgårds writings, including a brief biography, his most important articles, essays and theoretical writings during the 20 year period covered, analyses of several of his works by other authors, and a concluding essay by Per Nørgård. Includes a thorough discography and comprehensive bibliography of articles, books, interviews, reviews and analyses of his works through 1982.

B37.   Hansen, Ivan and Per Nørgård. *Trommebogen*. Copenhagen: Edition Wilhelm Hansen, 1982.

Ivan Hansen (percussionist, vocalist and writer specializing in contemporary music) and Per Nørgård discuss rhythm and percussion in modern music.

B38.   Hanson, Sten, ed. *Nordiska Musikfester/Nordic Music Days: 100 Years*. Stockholm: Kungl. Musikaliska akademien, 1988. 251 p.

Collection of essays on topics concerning contemporary music in Scandinavia in celebration of 100 years of the Nordic Music Days festival. Includes programs (with composers and titles) from every festival concert up to and including 1984.

B39.   Haven, Mogens von. *Balletten danser ud; billeder fra den Kongelige Danske ballet*. Intro. by John Martin. Copenhagen: Gyldendal, 1961. 112 p.

Photo-essay of the Royal Danish Ballet.

B40.   Haven, Mogens von. *The Royal Danish Ballet*. 2nd ed. Intro. by John Martin. Trans. Maureen Neiiendam. Copenhagen: Gyldendal, 1964. 120 p.

Translation of *Balletten danser ud* (*see* B39).

B41. Holm, Sven. *Vorten i Rued Langgaards ansigt. Funderinger over Rued Langgaard og hans ellevte symfoni.* Svaneke: np., 1995. 5 p.

Discusses Langgaard and the unusual story behind the many subtitles he gave his 11th symphony. Available from MIC. Also published in full on the Langgaard website (*see* R91).

B42. Holmboe, Vagn. *Det Uforklarlige.* Copenhagen: Gyldendal, 1981.

Excellent essay by the composer on music from the society's, composer's, performer's, and listener's viewpoints, as well as the "inexplicable" nature of music. English translation is found in *Experiencing Music: A Composer's Notes* (*see* B43).

B43. Holmboe, Vagn. *Experiencing Music: A Composer's Notes.* Trans. and ed. Paul Rapoport. London: Toccata Press, 1991. 138 p.

A collection of the most important essays and writings by Vagn Holmboe translated into English. Includes introduction and brief biography of the composer by Paul Rapoport, as well as a select bibliography of writings by and on Holmboe.

B44. Holmboe, Vagn. "On form and metamorphosis." *The Modern Composer and His World.* Eds. John Beckwith and Udo Kasemets. Toronto: University of Toronto Press, 1961. 134-40.

The composer discusses the compositional process and his theory of "metamorphosis" as it relates to thematic variation and form.

B45. Holmboe, Vagn and Meta Holmboe. *Samklang.* Copenhagen: Grafodan, 1980.

A collection of photos by Meta Holmboe, each accompanied by a full-page musical excerpt from various works of the composer.

B46. Horton, John. *Hokuo no ongaku.* Trans. Shozo Otsuka. Tokyo: Tokai-daigaku Shuppankai, 1971. 234 p.

Translation of *Scandinavian Music; a Short History* (*see* B47). In Japanese.

B47. Horton, John. *Scandinavian Music; a Short History.* London: Faber and Faber, 1963. 180 p.

A general overview of music in Scandinavia from the Middle Ages through the present. One chapter on "Danish Music since Carl Nielsen."

B48. Hvidtfeldt Nielsen, Svend. *Virkeligheden fortæller mig altid flere historier.* 2 vols. Odense: Det Fynske Musikkonservatorium, 1996. 262 p.
Ambitious overview of the theories, compositional processes, and "world views" of Per Nørgård. Technical, and assumes a fair amount of prior knowledge about Nørgård's work. Interesting and thorough (though somewhat esoteric) analyses of *Helle Nacht* and *Symphony No. 5.* Numerous musical examples, bibliography. Includes 60 page volume of musical excerpts.

B49. Jacobsen, Ejnar and Vagn Kappel. *Musikkens mestre; dansk komponister.* 2 vols. Copenhagen: Jul Gjellerup, 1944-1947.

"Photos, biographical details, long musical examples; no actual lists of works."[3]

B50. Jensen, Jørgen I. "A Sense of Form and Clandestine Meetings with Expressionism: Issues in Danish Music." *Nordiska Musikfester/Nordic Music Days: 100 Years.* Ed. Sten Hanson. Stockholm: Kungl. Musikaliska akademien, 1988. 9-28.

Excellent article covering the influential composers and important developments in Denmark in a semi-historical structure. Discusses the topics of continuity and expressionism within Danish music in this century.

B51. Jensen, Jørgen I. *Per Nørgårds Musik: et verdensbillede i forandring.* Copenhagen: Amadeus, 1986. 307 p.

Comprehensive book about Per Nørgård. Thorough discussion and analyses of Nørgård's theories and major works with numerous musical examples.

B52. Jensen, Jørgen I. *Per Nørgårds Third Symphony: A Short Introduction.* Trans. John Bergsagel. Copenhagen: Edition Wilhelm Hansen, 1977. 16 p.

Brief introduction to Nørgård's theory of hierarchal music and use of the Golden Mean and the infinity row, followed by a concise analysis of the third symphony. Much is either quoted directly or condensed from Nørgård's "Inside a Symphony" (*see* B436). Musical examples.

B53. Jensen, Niels Martin. "Denmark: 20th Century." *The New Grove Dictionary of Music and Musicians*. Ed. Stanlie Sadie. 20 vols. London: Macmillan, 1980. 5: 369-370.

Concise overview of all aspects of musical life regarding art-music in this century. Includes recent trends, important composers, list of Danish musical societies and organizations, bibliography.

B54. Jensen, Niels Martin. "Høffding, (Niels) Finn." *The New Grove Dictionary of Music and Musicians*. Ed. Stanlie Sadie. 20 vols. London: Macmillan, 1980. 8: 615-16.

Biographical profile of the composer. Selective work list, bibliography.

B55. Jensen, Niels Martin. "Jersild, Jørgen." *The New Grove Dictionary of Music and Musicians*. Ed. Stanlie Sadie. 20 vols. London: Macmillan, 1980. 9: 607-8.

Biographical profile of the composer. Selective work list, bibliography.

B56. Jensen, Niels Martin. "Riisager, Knudåge." *The New Grove Dictionary of Music and Musicians*. Ed. Stanlie Sadie. 20 vols. London: Macmillan, 1980. 16: 23-24.

Biographical profile of the composer. Selective work list, bibliography.

B57. Jersild, Jørgen, and Niels Viggo Bentzon, Jürgen Balzer. *Stilretninger i den nyere Tids Musik*. Copenhagen: Det unge tonekunstnerselskab, 1945. 36 p.

Three essays on the stylistic trends and important composers in the beginning of the century. Though not specifically about Danish music, it is interesting in that two of the authors (Jersild and

Bentzon) went on to become important composers in the decades that followed.

B58.   Johansen, Jens. *Seadrift*. Music Analysis No. 6., Nordic Music and Musicology in the 1970's. Nordic Music Research Conference, June 25-30th, 1979. Göteborg, 1979. 15 p.

Analysis of Per Nørgård's *Seadrift*, composed for the Danish early music ensemble Sub Rosa.

B59.   Kappel, Vagn. *Contemporary Danish Composers Against the Background of Danish Musical Life and History*. 3rd ed. Copenhagen: Det Danske Selskab, 1967. 116 p.

Concise summary of Danish musical history, with an emphasis on the second half of the 19th century. Short yet informative biographies on composers of this century. Especially valuable for composers of the generation of Carl Nielsen and those of the generation immediately following. Includes musical examples from each composer, photos, and lists of main works. A short section on recent musical life in Denmark.

B60.   Kappel, Vagn. *Danish Music from the Lur to the Vibraphone: Carl Nielsen and Modern Composers*. Copenhagen: Det Danske Selskab, 1951. 69 p.

Divided into two sections, each containing biographical sketches of several composers of Nielsen's generation and the generation immediately following, as well as very brief commentary of a particular work. Composers included Holmboe, Jersild, Bentzon, Schultz, Riisager, Koppel, Weis, Nielsen, Gade, and others.

B61.   Ketting, Knud, ed. *Music in Denmark*. Trans. Michael Chesnutt. Copenhagen: Det Danske Selskab, 1987. 111 p.

An overview of music in Denmark from art-music through jazz and folk. Includes biographies of several contemporary composers and a survey of recent developments and musical trends since Carl Nielsen. Non-scholarly tone aimed primarily at the popular audience. Selected bibliography.

B62.   Kinnunen Bruun, Sinikka. *Tanskalainen galoppi: 21 kulttuurivaikuttajaa taiteen eri aloilta*. Savonlinna: Savonlinnan

Kirjapaino, 1983.

A survey of 21 contemporary composers. Includes a chapter on
Vagn Holmboe, with an analysis of his 11th symphony. In Finnish.

B63.   Knudsen, Inge and Bent Olsen, eds. *Nogle danske komponister.*
Copenhagen: Danmarks skoleradio/TV, 1970. 68 p.

A collection of eight essays about Danish composers originally
compiled for use in an educational broadcast series for public
schools. Includes bibliographical references and insert about Per
Nørgård's "Infinity Row" theory.

B64.   Kragh-Jacobsen, Svend. *Balletten 1945-52.* Copenhagen: Areté,
1955. 113 p.

Overview of the activities of the Royal Danish Ballet from 1945-52.
Includes list of works performed. Brief mention of contemporary
Danish composers, esp. Knudåge Riisager.

B65.   Kragh-Jacobsen, Svend and Torben Krogh, eds. *Den Kongelige
Danske ballet.* Copenhagen: Selskabet til udgivelse af
kulturskrifter, 1952. 517 p.

Extensive overview of the history and repetoire of The Royal Danish
Ballet. Many illustrations, facsimiles, musical examples.

B66.   Kragh-Jacobsen, Svend. *The Royal Danish Ballet, an Old Tradition
and a Living Present.* Copenhagen: Det Danske Selskab, 1955.

Follow-up to the ambitious *Den Kongelige Danske ballet*, with a
focus on contemporary repertoire.

B67.   Kristensen, Sven Møller. *Den kødelige rationalisme: digtning,
musik, opdragelse, kultursociologi: artikler og vers 1936-79.*
Copenhagen: Gyldendal, 1979. 235 p.

B68.   Krogh, Torben. *Dansk Komponist-Forenings 25 Aars Jubilæum.*
Copenhagen: Dansk Komponistforening, 1939. 36 p.

B69.   Krummacher, Friedheim. *Musik im Norden. Abhandlungen über
skandinavische und norddeutsche Musik.* Bärenreiter-Verlag, 1996.
248 p.

B70.   Kruuse-Andersen, O. *Dansk Musiker Forbund gennem femogtyve Aar.* Copenhagen: Dansk Musiker Forbund, 1936. 80 p.

B71.   Kullberg, Erling. "De stormfulde år i dansk musik: Påvirkninger, holdninger og debat i det dansk kunstmusikliv i 10-året 1955-65." *Otte ekkoer af musikforskning i   Århus.* Århus: Musikvidenskabeligt Institut, 1988: 81-117.

A discussion of the "stormy years" in Danish music between 1955-1965. Focus on the controversy sparked when Per Nørgård, Ib Nørholm and Pelle Gudmundsen-Holmgreen visited Darmstadt and broke from the traditional æsthetics of Nielsen and Sibelius upon their return.

B72.   Kullberg, Erling. "Den hierarkiske musik." *Festskrift til Otto Mortensen på 70-årsdagen den 18. august 1977: fra kolleger og tidligere studerende ved Musikvidenskabeligt Institut, Aarhus Universitet.* Aarhus: Publimus, 1977.

Thorough, detailed essay on Per Nørgård's theories of hierarchic music, infinity series, and use of the Golden Mean. Many charts and musical examples. Appears in a slightly modified version as an article in *dmt* (*see* B388).

B73.   Kullberg, Erling. "Per Nørgård og den delte opmærksomhed. Et signalement af Nørgårds musik i dag med fokus på nogle af dens perceptuelle aspekter som de kommer til udtryk i violinkoncerten fra 1987." *Festskrift Søren Sørensen.* Eds. Finn Egeland Hansen et al. Copenhagen: Dan Fog, 1990. 135-156.

Excellent article covering the various style-periods of Per Nørgård, with a focus on the priciple of "selective perception." Brief analysis of the violin concerto *Helle Nacht* (1987), with a focus on this phenomenon. Musical examples, bibliography.

B74.   Larsen, Karl, ed. *Levende Musik - Mekanisk Musik.* Copenhagen: Dansk Tonekunstnerforening, 1931. 56 p.

A rather quaint discussion of the repercussions that "mechanical music" (i.e., radio and grammophone) was believed to have on music, "unemploying countless musicians," among others. Contributions by composers Finn Høffding and Jørgen Bentzon with a preface by Carl Nielsen only months prior to his death.

B75.   Layton, Robert. "Vagn Holmboe and the later Scandinavians." *The Symphony.* Ed. Robert Simpson. Harmondsworth: Penguin Books, 1967. 2: 230-42.

Rather generalized, incomplete overview of 20th century composers in Scandinavia.

B76.   Leicth, Georg and Marianne Hallar. *Det Kongelige Teaters repertoire, 1889-1975.* Copenhagen: Bibliotekscentralens Forlag, 1977. 437 p.

"A chronology of all opera, drama and ballet performances in the national theater ... Lists of titles of works. Indexes of authors, composers, choreographers, designers and conductors."[4]

B77.   Lindhjem, Anna. *Kvinnelige komponister og musikk-skole-utgivere i Skandinavien.* Fredriksstad: Hanssens trykkeri og bokbinderi, 1931. 29 p.

B78.   Lunn, Sven, ed. *La vie musicale au Danemark.* Copenhagen: La Commission permanente des expositions à la Maison du Danemark à Paris, 1962. 135 p.

General overview of Danish music, musical life and music history. Of particular interest is the chapter by Tage Nielsen on Danish music and composers in the generation immediately following Carl Nielsen, and Svend Kragh-Jacobsen's chapter on Danish opera since 1931.

B79.   Lynge, Gerhardt. *Danske Komponister i det 20. Aarhundredes Begyndelse.* 2nd ed. Copenhagen: E.H. Jung, 1917. 279 p.

Comprehensive overview of Danish composers active in the early years of the century. Provides a good background to the musical scene in the decades to follow.

B80.   Magnussen, Jul. *Vor Tids danske Musikere og Tonekunstnere.* Copenhagen, 1937. 565 p.

B81.   Marschner, Bo. *Fra Levende Musik til musikæstetisk stillingskrig. Perspektiver i dansk musikæstetik i 1920'ern og begyndelsen af - 30'erne.* Handout from the seminar "Dansk musik i Carl Nielsen-tid," Musikvidenskabeligt Institut, Aarhus Universitet. (July/August,

1972). 25 p.

Discusses aesthetical developments and controversies within Danish musical life preceding and closely following the death of Carl Nielsen. Copies available from MIC.

B82. Marschner, Bo and Søren Sørensen, eds. *Gads musikhistorie.* Copenhagen: G.E.C. Gad, 1990. 612 p.

B83. Marschner, Bo. "Langgaard, Rued (Immanuel)." *The New Grove Dictionary of Music and Musicians.* Ed. Stanlie Sadie. 20 vols. London: Macmillan, 1980. 10: 450.

Biographical profile of the composer. Selective work list, bibliography.

B84. Marschner, Bo. *Rued Langgaard.* Århus: np., 1973. 22 p.

Informative, unpublished paper giving an overview of the life and work of Langgaard, with some emphasis on his use of symbolism in such works as his 7th and 11th symphonies and *Sfærernes Musik.*

B85. Mathisen, Oddvin. *Bogen om Poul Schierbeck.* Copenhagen: Busck, 1988. 449 p.

Biography and study of the works of Poul Schierbeck within the context of Danish musical life. Includes complete list of works, musical exampes, illustrations.

B86. Mathisen, Oddvin. *En oversigt over Poul Schierbecks liv og værker, samt en analyse af hans enstemmige sange med klaverledsagelse for at klargøre brug af de musikalske virkemidler.* MA thesis, University of Copenhagen, 1972. 352 p.

"A survey of the life and works of Poul Schierbeck, and an analysis of his solo songs with piano accompaniment for the purpose of clarifying his musical style." Reviews various biographical materials, discusses Schierbeck's style and instrumentation, and analyses all of his songs for solo voice. Includes catalogue of works, illustration, portrait, music examples, discography.

B87. McLoskey, Lansing D. *Forskelligheder: Diversity in Danish 20th Century Music. A Discussion of Stylistic Plurality; or, "Don't tell me what to do!"* Cupertino, CA: Odhecaton Z Music, 1996. 18 p.

Discusses the topic of diversity in 20th century Danish music. Considers various reasons for this stylistic multiplicity, the ways in which it manifests itself, and provides an historical backdround for the state of art-music in Denmark.

B88.   McLoskey, Lansing D. *Publications on 20th Century Art-music in Denmark in the Post-Nielsen Era (1931-present).* Cupertino, CA: Odhecaton Z Music, 1996. Presented at the National Conference of SASS (The Society for the Advancement of Scandinavian Study), William & Mary College, Williamsburg, VA. (May, 1996). 27 p.

Overview of the current state of research and publication in the field of 20th century Danish music, including important authors and publishers in the field, trends in publication and topics, the dissemi- nation of materials, music and recordings, and *lacunæ* in the field.

B89.   Meyer, Torben and Josef Müller-Marein, Hannes Reinhardt, eds. *Musikalske selvportrætter.* Copenhagen: Gjellerup, 1966. 325 p.

Collection of brief autobiographical sketches, including several Danish composers.

B90.   *Mindeskrift over Jørgen Bentzon.* Copenhagen: np., 1957. 54 p.

A *festschrift* prepared by some of Bentzon's colleagues and former students, honoring the composer on what would have been his 60th birthday (Bentzon died six years earlier). Includes an informative article by Finn Høffding. Complete list of works, photos, letter facsimiles.

B91.   Moore, David Arthur. *Per Nørgårds Spell for Clarinet, 'Cello and Piano: An Analysis.* Ph. D. dissertation, Eastman School of Music. Rochester, NY: Eastman School of Music, 1986. 45 p.

Thorough analysis of *Spell* (1973), with numerous charts and musical examples. Also includes a concise yet informative basic explanation of the infinity row theory. Extensive bibliography.

B92.   Mortensen, Jørgen. *Per Nørgårds Tonesøer.* Esbjerg: Vestjysk Musikkonservatorium, 1993. 146 p.

Study of Per Nørgård's compositional techniques, in particular his theory of "tone seas." Extensive musical examples. Includes epilogue by the composer.

B93. Mortensen, Jørgen. *Rapport om projekt: Den Elektroniske Musikskole.* Esbjerg: Vestjysk Musikkonservatorium, 1995. 64 p.

Describes the activity and results of the experimental education program "The Electronic Music School." In the project, students residing in different parts of Denmark studied composition and other music courses via modem and computer with the instructor and project leader, Jørgen Mortensen.

B94. Møldrup, Erling. *Guitaren. Et eksotisk instrument i den danske musik.* Copenhagen: Edition Kontrapunkt, 1997. 279 p.
General overview of the history of the role of the guitar in Danish music up until 1960, with a discussion of prominent figures and important works. Includes a full-length CD with musical examples.

B95. *Munksgaards musik leksikon.* Copenhagen: Munksgaard, 1965. 269 p.

B96. *Music from Denmark, Norway and Sweden: The Young Generations.* 2nd ed. Copenhagen: Edition Wilhelm Hansen, 1968. 31 p.

Biographies of 25 contemporary composers and lists of their works published by Edition Wilhelm Hansen.

B97. *Music in Copenhagen. Studies in the Musical Life of Copenhagen in the 19th and 20th Centuries.* Copenhagen: Musikvidenskabeligt Institut, 1996. 299 p.

Special English edition of the yearbook of the Musikvidenskabeligt Institut, normally titled *Musik & forskning.* It is the culmination of a three-year research project at the institute. Includes articles on topics from 1800 through the 1970's, with an emphasis on the first half of the 19th century. Excellent article on the composer Jørgen Bentzon, active in the first half of the century.

B98. *Musikkens hvem hvad hvor biografier.* 2 vols. Copenhagen: Politikens forlag, 1961.

Very brief biographies of important musical figures from all eras and nationalities, with an emphasis on Scandinavian musicians. Includes short selective work list for composers.

B99. Maegaard, Jan, and Per Nørgård, Jens Østergaard. *Lyt til musikken.* Copenhagen: Danmarks Radio, 1971.

B100. Maegaard, Jan. *Musikalsk modernisme, 1945-1962.* 2nd ed. Copenhagen: Willhelm Hansen, 1971. 133 p.

B101. Maegaard, K., ed. *Musica danese.* Rome: Donazione Augustinus Fonden, 1985. 67 p.

B102. Nesheim, Elef. "Scandinavian Musical Exoticism." *Nordiska Musikfester/Nordic Music Days: 100 Years.* Ed. Sten Hanson. Stockholm: Kungl. Musikaliska akademien, 1988. 41-60.

An interesting study of the percentage of Nordic music composed after 1950 that is performed and broadcast in the various Scandinavian countries.

B103. Nielsen, Poul *Dansk musik.* Copenhagen: Dansk-Norsk Fond, 1968. 80 p.

B104. Nielsen, Tage. *Danish Music after Carl Nielsen.* Copenhagen: 1962. 12 p.

Overview of important composers and musical trends in Denmark in the decades following the death of Nielsen. Appeared slightly revised as an article in *Music Journal (see* B426).

B105. *Ny musik i Norden.* Stockholm: Föreningen Norden, 1953. 142 p.

A collaboration between the Scandinavian countries as part of a series of publications on a variety of topics ranging from politics and science to literature and history. Contains chapters on contemporary music in each of the five countries. Excellent bibliographies and discographies for each country.

B106. Nørgård, Per. "Flugten til Århus. Bidrag til forståelse af 'Århus-miljøet for ny musik' siden 1965." *Festskrift Søren Sørensen.* Eds. Finn Egeland Hansen et al. Copenhagen: Dan Fog, 1990. 295-98.

Discussion of the atmosphere and controversy surrounding the attitudes towards new music and experimental ideas in Copenhagen (esp. the Royal Danish Conservatory of Music) vs. Aarhus in the mid-60's up to the present.

B107. Nørgård, Per. *Hierarkisk genesis: trin henimod en naturlig musikteori? Musikopleven som interferens mellem forventning og realisering.* Copenhagen: Per Nørgård, 1977.

Lengthy essay on his theory of hierarchy within musical structure and discussion of the musical experience in terms of expectation vs. realization. Translation found in *Dansk Aarbog for Musikforskning.* XIV, 1983 (*see* B434).

B108. Nørgård, Per. *Kompendium over metoder og studier i en ny kompositorisk teknik og tænkemåde.* Copenhagen: Per Nørgård, 1972.

"Commentary about his own compositions and compositional techniques during the period from 1959-72 with a focus on 1970-72."[5]

B109. Nørgård, Per. *Rued Langgaards lange kamp - mod de forkerte..."* Copenhagen: Per Nørgård, 1993. 3 p.

Opening remarks at the opening of the Royal Danish Libary's exhibit in commemoration of Langgaard's 100th birthday, given on Sept. 9, 1993. Available from MIC.

B110. Nørholm, Ib and Poul Borum. *Modskabelse: et digt.* Århus: Jorinde & Joringel, 1979. 33 p.

Text, commentary and analysis of Nørholms 4th symphony, commissioned by Copenhagen University and performed at the University's 500th anniversary celebration.

B111. Otsuka, Shozo. "Denmahku: Nihlusen igo." *Ongakudaijiten 3.* Ed. Hiroshi Shimonaka. Tokyo: Heibonsha, 1982. 1592-1593.

"Denmark: After Nielsen." Entry in the music encyclopedia *Ongakudaijiten 3* by the Japanese musicologist Shozo Otsuka, who also translated John Horton's *Scandinavian Music; a Short History* (*see* B46).

B112. Pade, Steen. "Landsdelsorkesterproblemer." *Festskrift Søren Sørensen.* Eds. Finn Egeland Hansen et al. Copenhagen: Dan Fog, 1990. 299-310.

Discussion of the problems in programming, administrating and financing the national symphony orchestras in Denmark.

B113. Pedersen, Peder Kaj. "Bernhard Christensen: En jazzinflueret komponist? En undersøgelse af nogle tidlige værker." *Col Legno.* Vol. 1. Ed. Finn Egeland Hansen. Aalborg: Aalborg Universitet and Nordjysk Musikkonservatorium, 1992. 205 p.

B114. Petersen, Frede Schandorf. "Status over et halvsekel." *Ny musik i Norden.* Stockholm: Föreningen Norden, 1954. 7-42.

Excellent, detailed overview of musical developements and composers in Denmark from 1900-50, including a historical background of the late 19th century. Includes brief bios and subjective critiques of selected works from each composer.

B115. Rapoport, Paul. *Opus est: Six Composers from Northern Europe.* London: Kahn and Averill, 1978. 200 p.

Includes a chapter on Vagn Holmboe, with an analysis of *Symphony No. 7.*

B116. Rapoport, Paul. *Vagn Holmboe: A Catalog of Works and Recordings with Indexes of Persons and Titles..* 3rd ed. Copenhagen: Edition Wilhelm Hansen,   1996. 224 p.

See B198.

B117. Rapoport, Paul. *Vagn Holmboe's Symphonic Metamorphoses.* Ph.D. dissertation, University of Illinois. Urbana, IL: University of Illinois, 1975.

B118. Rasmussen, Karl Aage and Jesper Hørn. *Noteworthy Danes: Portraits of Eleven Danish Composers.* Trans. by author. Copenhagen: Edition Wilhelm Hansen, 1991. 118 p.

English translation of *Toneangivende danskere: 11 Komponistportrætter i tekst og billeder* (*see* B119).

B119. Rasmussen, Karl Aage and Jesper Hørn. *Toneangivende danskere: 11 Komponistportrætter i tekst og billeder.* Copenhagen: Edition Wilhelm Hansen, 1991. 118 p.

Brief biographies of eleven of the most prominent Danish composers in the second half of the 20th century with portraits of each composer by photographer Jesper Hørn. Selective work lists and discographies.

B120. Rasmussen, Pia. "Frauen machen Musik." *Island, Grönland, Dänemark und die Faröer der Frauen.* Eds. Birthe Marker, Lene Sjorup and Karen Wolf. Transl. Ulla Weber and Jornun Sigurdardottir. Munich: Frauenoffensive, 1991.

B121. Ravnkilde, Svend, ed. *Den 3. Komponistbiennale; Programbog.* Copenhagen: Dansk Komponist Forening, 1996. 145 p.

Program book for the Young Composers 1960-1996/3rd Composer's Biennale Music Festival sponsored by the Danish Composers' Society. In addition to the complete program with notes for the entire festival, the booklet includes biographical notes for numerous Danish and Scandinavian composers, three brief yet excellent essays on Danish music, and several photos and illustrations.

B122. Ravnkilde, Svend, ed. *The 3rd Composers' Biennale; Programme Book.* Copenhagen: Dansk Komponist Forening, 1996. 145 p.

English edition of *Den 3. Komponistbiennale; Programbog (see* B121).

B123. Reynolds, William H. "Berg, Gunnar (Johnsen)." *The New Grove Dictionary of Music and Musicians.* Ed. Stanlie Sadie. 20 vols. London: Macmillan, 1980. 2: 538-39.

Biographical profile of the composer. Selective work list, bibliography.

B124. Reynolds, William H. "Borup-Jørgensen, (Jens) Axel." *The New Grove Dictionary of Music and Musicians.* Ed. Stanlie Sadie. 20 vols. London: Macmillan, 1980. 3: 71-72.

Biographical profile of the composer. Selective work list, bibliography.

B125. Reynolds, William H. "Koppel, Herman D(avid)." *The New Grove Dictionary of Music and Musicians.* Ed. Stanlie Sadie. 20 vols. London: Macmillan, 1980. 10: 186.

Biographical profile of the composer. Selective work list, bibliography.

B126. Reynolds, William H. "Nørgård, Per." *The New Grove Dictionary of Music and Musicians.* Ed. Stanlie Sadie. 20 vols. London: Macmillan, 1980. 13: 279-80.

Biographical profile of the composer. Selective work list, bibliography.

B127. Reynolds, William H. "Nørholm Ib." *The New Grove Dictionary of Music and Musicians.* Ed. Stanlie Sadie. 20 vols. London: Macmillan, 1980. 13: 280-82.

Biographical profile of the composer. Selective work list, bibliography.

B128. Riisager, Knudåge. *Det er sjovt at være lille.* Copenhagen: Forfatteren, 1967. 12 p.

B129. Riisager, Knudåge. *Det usynliger mønster.* Copenhagen: Nyt nordisk Forlag, 1957. 176 p.

A collection of 15 essays by the composer published in honor of his 60th birthday. Although not about Danish music, the book provides interesting insight into Riisager as a person and prolific writer, with topics ranging from music and art to science and his pet cat.

B130. Riisager, Knudåge. *Tanker i tiden.* Copenhagen: C. Andersen, 1952. 27 p.

B131. Rossel, J. "Gunnar Berg: *Pierres solaires.*" *Festskrift til Arne Kjær.* Aarhus: Peters forlag, 1973. 55.

B132. *Samfundet til udgivelse af dansk musik, 1871-1971.* Copenhagen: Samfundet, 1971. 158 p.

Report of the history and activities of Samfundet in commemoration of the 100th anniversary of the organization. Brief essays by several

Danish composers and musicologists. Includes a summary of the entire book in English by John Bergsagel.

B133. Schepelern, Gerhard. *Operaens historie i Danmark 1634-1975.* Copenhagen: Munksgaard/Rosinante, 1995. 366 p.

Longtime Danish opera critic Gerhard Schepelern's ambitious work covering the complete history of opera in Denmark, focusing on repertoire and presenters. A large part of the book - all chapters about productions and singers from the 1930's to 1975- are written in the first person. Written on the colloquial side, the book contains more subjective opinions than most scholarly reference sources.

B134. Schepelern, Gerhard and Gereon Brodin. "Rud Langgaard 1893-1952" and "*Sfinx* - Tonebillede for stort Orkester." *Koncerthaandbogen.* Copenhagen: Jul Gjellerup, 1956-59. 3: 250-54.

B135. Schiørring, Nils. "Dänemark." *Die Musik in Geschichte und Gegenwart; allgemeine Enzyklopädie der Musik.* Ed. Friedrich Blume. Kassel: Bärenreiter-Verlag, 1949-.

Overview of art-music in historical perspective. 20th century music, concert life, musical examples.

B136. Schiørring, Nils. *Musikkens historie in Danmark.* Eds. Ole Kongsted, P.H. Traustedt. 3 vols. Copenhagen: Politikens Forlag, 1977-78. 1,100+ p.

Covers the history of art music from Middle Ages to 1970's in general, unfootnoted narrative. Some attention to folk music. 3rd volume has rather incomplete coverage of 20th century.

B137. Schiørring, Nils. *Musikkens veje.* Copenhagen: Berlingske forlag, 1959. 160 p.

B138. Schiørring, Nils. "Musikkens 1951 - Nogle retninger i nutidig dansk tonekunst." Hefte udgivet af Gutenberghus, 1951. 32-40.

B139. Schwartz, Elliott and Daniel Godfrey. *Music Since 1945: Issues, Materials, and Literature.* New York: Schirmer Books, 1993. 537 p.

Concise yet informative synopsis of the important developments and composers since the Second World War. Includes brief analysis of Per Nørgård's *Symphony No. 3*.

B140. Searle, Humphrey and Robert Layton. *Twentieth Century Composers: Britain, Scandinavia and the Netherlands*. Ed. Nicolas Nabokov and Anna Kallin. *Twentieth Century Composers*. 3 vols. London: Weidenfeld and Nicolson, 1972. Vol 3. 200 p.

Very incomplete coverage for Scandinavian countries (only 45 pages for all five countries). Primarily Sibelius and Nielsen. One brief and very incomplete chapter on Scandinavian composers since Sibelius.

B141. Slonimsky, Nicolas, ed. *Baker's Biographical Dictionary of Musicians*. 8th edition. New York: Schirmer Books, 1992. 2,115 p.

Historic and important reference guide of musicians from all eras, fields, and regions, in the form of brief biographical sketches. Most of the central figures in Danish music of this century are included, most often with a list of their most important works.

B142. Sørensen, Søren, and John Christiansen, Finn Slumstrup, eds. *Gads musikleksikon*. 2nd ed. 2 vols. Copenhagen: Gad, 1987. 366 p. Definitive Danish dictionary of music. Includes coverage of most of the important Danish composers, musicians, conductors, theories, and Danish musical life.

B143. Steensen, Steen Christian. "Ib Nørholm - *Sandhedens hævn*." *Pipers Enzyklopädie des Musiktheaters*. Ed. Carl Dahlhaus. 5 vols. Munich: Forschungsinstitut für Musiktheater der Universität Bayreuth, 1989. 4: 466-68.

Description and overview of the opera. Photo.

B144. Steensen, Steen Christian. "Per Nørgård - *Gilgamesh*." *Pipers Enzyklopädie des Musiktheaters*. Ed. Carl Dahlhaus. 5 vols. Munich: Forschungsinstitut für Musiktheater der Universität Bayreuth, 1989. 4: 465-66.

Description and overview of the opera. Photo.

B145. Tagung, Kieler. *Gattung und Werk in der Musikgeschichte Norddeutschlands und Skandinaviens.* Kassel: Barenreiter, 1982. 179 p.

B146. Thimus, Albert Freiherr von. *Die harmonikale Symbolik des Altherthums.* 2 vols. New York: Hildesheim, 1972.

Reprint of the seminal treatise on modern speculative musical theory, originally published in 1876. Though not about Danish music, it is noteworthy in that it was a powerful influence on Per Nørgård during the 1970's, especially regarding the development of his theories concerning the harmonic series, "undertones," and their symbolism.

B147. Thybo, Leif. *Lærebog i improvisation.* Copenhagen: Edition Wilhelm Hansen, 1956.

Although not specifically about Danish music, it is noteworthy in that it is the earliest book about musical improvisation written in Denmark. The current musical climate was fairly conservative and improvisation was considered rather avant-garde at the time.

B148. Vestergaard, Mogens, ed. *Fra byorkester til symfoniorkester: Odense Symfoniorkester 1946-96.* Odense: Odense Symfoniorkester, 1996. 176 p.

B149. Viinholt Nielsen, Bendt. "Pettersson und Langgaard: Zwei 'komplementäre Aussenseiter'." Ed. Michael Mäckelman. *Allan Pettersson Jahrbuch 1987.* Frankfurt: International Allan Pettersson Gesellschaft, 1987. 46-59.

B150. Viinholt Nielsen, Bendt. "Rued Langgaard - *Antikrist*, Kirke-opera." *Pipers Enzyklopädie des Musiktheaters.* Ed. Carl Dahlhaus. 5 vols. Munich: Forschungsinstitut für Musiktheater der Universität Bayreuth, 1989. 3: 411-12.

B151. Viinholt Nielsen, Bendt. *Rued Langgaard; Biografi.* Copenhagen: Engstrøm & Sødring, 1993. 334 p.

Definitive, comprehensive biography of the Danish "outsider" Rued Immanual Langgaard by the preeminent Langgaard authority Viinholt Nielsen. Musical examples, photos, description of cultural and musical contexts.

B152. Wallner, Bo. "Modern Music in Scandinavia." *European Music in the Twentieth Century.* Ed. Howard Hartog. London: Routledge and Kegan Paul, Ltd., 1957. 118-131.

General overview of Scandinavian music, with approximately three pages focusing on Denmark.

B153. Wallner, Bo. *Scandinavian Composers of Our Time.* Stockholm: Nordiska Musikförlaget, 1973.

"Biographical information on composers active since 1920, with extensive bibliographies and documents."[6]

B154. Wallner, Bo. "Scandinavian Music after the Second World War." *Contemporary Music in Europe.* Ed. Paul Henry Lang and Nathan Broder. New York: G. Schirmer, Inc., 1965. 111-143.

B155. Wallner, Bo. *Scandinavian Music after the Second World War.* Stockholm: Nordiska Musikförlaget, nd.

"Prominent composers and trends in Scandinavia. Five Danish composers discussed in some depth. Good survey of writings about Danish Music."[7]

B156. Wallner, Bo. *Vär tids musik i Norden; från 20-tal till 60-tal.* Stockholm: Nordiska Musikförlaget, 1968. 435 p.

Overview of Scandinavian composers and general musical life from the 1920s into the 1960s. Includes discography, portraits, musical examples, bibliography, and some primary sources (such as letters). In Swedish.

B157. Wellejus, Th. *End er der Sang i Skoven: Vore danske Tonekunstnere.* Slagelse: np., 1941. 195 p.

B158. Wind, Tage. *Joen Waagstein.* Copenhagen: Gyldendal, 1952. 75 p.

Biography of the pioneering Faroese composer, organist, teacher and painter Joen Waagstein.

B159. Yoell, John H. *The Nordic Sound; Explorations into the Music of Denmark, Norway and Sweden.* Boston: Crescendo Publishing Company, 1974. 264 p.

Good general overview of Scandinavian music history. Includes discography and program notes on recordings by 43 Nordic composers; many of them being from the 20th century. Brief biographies from personal interviews with the composers.

Bibliographies and Catalogues

B160. Balzer, Jürgen. *Bibliographie des compositeurs danois.*
Copenhagen: Dansk Komponistforening, 1932. 64 p.

B161. Balzer, Jürgen. *Bibliografi over dansk komponister.* Copenhagen:
Dansk Komponistforening, 1932. 64 p.

B162. Berg, Sigurd and Svend Bruhns. *Knudåge Riisagers Kompositioner.*
Copenhagen: Dansk Komponist-Forening, 1967. 48 p.

Catalogue of works by the composer Knudåge Riisager.

B163. Berg, Sigurd. *Fortegnelse over danske forfatteres bøger og piecer
vedrørende personer med tilknytning til musiklivet ...* Copenhagen:
Bibliotekscentralen, 1944.

As the title implies, it is a "List of books and pamphlets by Danish
authors and about people associated with [Danish] musical life, and
similar works by foreign authors as long as they are published in
Denmark or are about music in Denmark." Approx. 300 entries, not
annotated.

B164. Bjørnum, Birgit. *Per Nørgårds kompositioner 1949-82.*
Copenhagen: Edition Wilhelm Hansen, 1982. 247 p.

Chronological, comprehensive thematic catalogue of the works of
Per Nørgård. Includes discography.

B165. Bonfils, Kim, and Mikael Højris, Bendt Viinholt Nielsen, eds.
Music in Denmark; Key Directory '96. Copenhagen: Danish Music

Information Centre, 1995. 87 p.

Valuable pocketbook directory containing information, addresses and phone numbers for Danish organizations, companies and societies pertaining to music in Denmark. Includes publishers/distributors, management, venues, media, organizations, authorities, institutions, operas and orchestras, and Danish Cultural Institutes abroad. Also includes calender of selected musical events from *Kulturby 96* (Copenhagen '96, Cultural Capital of Europe).

B166. "Books and periodicals 1988; compiled by the Danish Music Information Centre." *Musical Denmark*. 41 (1989): 22.

B167. Bruhns, Svend and Dan Fog. *Finn Høffding: Komponistioner. En fortegnelse ved S.B. og D.F.* Copenhagen: Dan Fogs Musikforlag, 1969. 49 p.

B168. Bull, Storm. *Index to Biographies of Contemporary Composers*. 3 vols. New York: Scarecrow Press, 1964-87.

An index to biographies of contemporary composers, and includes most of the important figures in Danish music. Citings do not give a description of the reference - it may be a book, lengthy article on the composer, or simply an article where the composer's name happens to be mentioned in passing. Limited number of non-English citings.

B169. Clausen, Per Groth, ed. *Dansk Musik; Katalog over Statsbibliotekets samling af trykte musikalier.* Aarhus: Universitetsforlaget, 1977. 316 p.

A catalogue of the Statsbiblioteket's collection of works by Danish composers as of Dec. 1975. Contains a great deal of contemporary music.

B170. *Dansk musikfortegnelse. 1931-71.* Copenhagen: Dansk Musik-handlerforening, 1972.

Catalogue of music deposited at the Royal Library and the State and University Library in Århus.

B171. *Dansk musikfortegnelse/The Danish National Bibliography; Music, 1976-.* Ballerup: The Danish Library Bureau, 1977-.

"Compiled by the Music Dept. of the Royal Library. Bibliography of music published abroad by Danes and music by any composer on Danish texts or otherwise related to Denmark. All scores and some books on music; about 400 entries per year. Title page and foreword in both English and Danish."[8]

B172. *Danske Komponister af idag; en værkfortegnelse. Danish Composers of Today; a Catalogue of works. Dänische Komponisten von heute; ein Werkverzeichnis.* Ed. Jens-Ole Malmgren. 2 vols. Copenhagen: Dansk Komponistforening, 1980.

An updated and revised catalogue of over 100 Danish composers and over 4500 works. Includes number of movements, instrumentation, duration, premiere date, publisher, commissioning institution. In Danish, English and German.

B173. Falk, Johan and Ann Hörnquist, eds. *NOMUS-Katalogen. The NOMUS Catalogue.* Stockholm: NOMUS, 1994. 168 p.

Valuable address and telephone register for music authorities, institutions, and organizations in the Scandinavian and Baltic countries. Includes public institutions, professional associations, orchestras, publications, periodicals, festivals and concert bureaus. Introduction in Swedish and English.

B174. Fanger, Eva-Brit. *Katalog over musiktidsskrifter i danske forskningsbiblioteker.* Copenhagen: Det Kgl. Bibliotek, 1997. 118 p.

A catalogue of music periodicals in Danish research libraries.

B175. "Finn Saverys værkliste." *dmt.* 55: 1 (Sept. 1980): 22-23.

Selective work list and discography for the composer Finn Savery.

B176. Fog, Dan and Jan Maegaard, eds. *Danish Music, Catalogue 1956.* Copenhagen: K. Larsen musikforlag, 1956. 64 p.

B177. Fog, Dan. *Dänische Musikverlage und Notendruckerien. Beiträge zur Musikaliendatierung.* Copenhagen: Dan Fog, 1972.

"Useful list of 60 publishers of music, with chronologies of events relating to their firms. Not a list of music published. Name index."[9]

B178. Fog, Dan. *The Royal Danish Ballet, 1760-1958, and August Bournonville; a chronological catalogue of the ballets and ballet-divertissements performed at the Royal Theatres of Copenhagen and a catalogue of Bournonville's works.* Copenhagen, Dan Fog, 1961. 78 p.

Includes illustrations, facsimiles, musical examples, and musical bibliography.

B179. Fog, Dan, ed. *Samfundet til udgivelse af Dansk musik.* Copenhagen: The Society for Publishing Danish Music, 1974.

Valuable reference source that includes catalogue of publications (all in Danish), a brief outline of Danish music history, biographical sketches of numerous composers, and an appendix with a list of prices for scores, parts and recordings published by The Society for Publishing Danish Music. In English.

B180. Hamburger, Povl. *Bibliografisk fortegnelse over Thomas Laubs litteraere og musikalske arbejder.* Copenhagen: Specialbogtrykkeriet, 1932. 46 p.

B181. Hansen, Ulla Spühler and Tine Vind. *Dansk kormusik 1975-85: en bibliografi.* Copenhagen: Danmarks biblioteksskole, 1985. 173 p.

Valuable reference source for Danish choral music from 1975 to 1985.

B182. Harbo, Nils, ed. *Dansk Musik Årbog.* Copenhagen: Dansk Musik Årbog ApS.

Directory containing information, addresses and phone numbers for all Danish organizations, companies and societies pertaining to music in Denmark. Includes instrument shops/makers, studios, TV and radio, music festivals, competitions/awards, concert halls and venues, educational institutions, record companies, music publishers, foundations, music libraries, orchestras and choirs, as well as current addresses and phone numbers for all members of aforementioned organizations (including most contemporary art-music composers). Published yearly.

B183. Henriksen, Inge, ed. *Music in Danish Libraries 1973, A Union Catalogue. Musikalier i danske biblioteker 1973,*

Accessionskatalog. Copenhagen: The Office of the National Librarian, 1974. 267 p.

A catalogue of foreign music as well as all printed Danish music at the Royal Library and the State and University Libraries not included in *Dansk musikfortegnelse. 1931-71.*

B184. Jensen, Jørgen I. *Bo Holten.* Copenhagen: Edition Wilhelm Hansen, c.1993. 8 p.

Work list and discography. Includes informative biographical profile of the composer and brief descriptions of important works.

B185. Johansen, Svend Aaquist. *Ib Nørholm.* Trans. Wayne Siegel. Copenhagen: Edition Wilhelm Hansen, 1985. 7 p.

Complete work list with discography. Includes biographical sketch and brief descriptions of important works. In pamphlet form.

B186. *Katalog over musik og musiklitteratur.* 5 vols. Copenhagen: Nordlunde, 1954-58.

Catalogue of music in the Copenhagen Commune Libraries. Of particular interest is vol. 5, which lists books on theory, music history and biographies.

B187. Ketting, Knud, ed. "Discover Nordic Brass Music: 150 Contemporary Nordic brass pieces." *Nordic Sounds.* (1988): 10-11.

B188. Ketting, Knud, ed. *Discover Nordic Choral Music.* Copenhagen: NOMUS, 1987. 8 p.

Special issue of *Nordic Sounds.*

B189. Ketting, Knud, ed. *Discover Nordic Piano Music.* Copenhagen: NOMUS, 1991. 8 p.

Special issue of *Nordic Sounds.*

B190. Ketting, Knud, ed. *Discover Nordic String Quartets.* Copenhagen: NOMUS, 1990. 8 p.

Special issue of *Nordic Sounds.* Includes brief commentary by Vagn Holmboe.

B191. *Mindeskrift over Jørgen Bentzon.* Copenhagen: np., 1957. 54 p.

See B90.

B192. Mortensen, Tore. *Otto Mortensen - En værkfortegnelse.*
Copenhagen: Dan Fog, 1993. 80 p.

B193. Møllerhøj, Klaus. *Niels Viggo Bentzons Kompositioner.*
Copenhagen: Edition Wilhelm Hansen, 1980. 160 p.

A complete register of the works of Niels Viggo Bentzon from 1939
through 1979 (400+ works). Listed first by opus number, with
indexes by instrumentation and title. Includes selective discography.

B194. Nørgaard, Felix and Harald Krabs, Waldemar Wolsing, eds. *De
Musiske udsendelser: DR 1925-1975: radioteater, musik, TVteater.*
2 vols. Copenhagen: Nyt Nordisk Forlag, 1975-

B195. Nørgård, Per. *List of works.* Copenhagen: Edition Wilhelm Hansen,
1976.

List of works with brief descriptions by the composer. In pamphlet
form.

B196. Olsen, Henning Smidth. "Music in the Danish National
Bibliography." *Fontes Artis Musicæ.* 34.2,3 (1987): 90+.

Abstracts in English, German and French.

B197. Olt, Harry. *Musiklivet i Norden.* Copenhagen: Ministeriet for
Kulturelle Anliggender, 1969. 74 p.

A directory of musical institutions and events in Scandinavia. Lists
of orchestras and other performing groups, festivals, broadcasting,
music libraries and periodicals. For more accurate, up-to-date
information, refer instead to the *NOMUS Katalog, Dansk Musik
Årbog,* or *Music in Denmark; Key Directory '96* (see respective
listings).

B198. Rapoport, Paul. *Vagn Holmboe: A Catalog of Works and
Recordings with Indexes of Persons and Titles.* 3rd ed.
Copenhagen: Edition Wilhelm Hansen, 1996. 224 p.

A comprehensive and detailed catalogue of the music of Vagn

Holmboe, including titles, dates, instrumentation, publisher, language, and first performance dates. Also includes a complete discography of recordings, a selective bibliography of articles by and about Holmboe, and translations of three important essays by Holmboe.

B199. Rasmussen, Jan William and Sven C. Jacobsen, eds. *Dania Polyglotta*. Copenhagen: Det kongelige Bibliotek, 1995. 242 p.

A bibliography compiled by the Danish Department of the Royal Library. Includes over 2,500 books and articles in 39 languages organized by topic. Excellent research guide, though far from comprehensive concerning music.

B200. Rasmussen, Karl Aage. *Per Nørgård.* Trans. Rosalind Bevan. Copenhagen: Edition Wilhelm Hansen, 1991. 10 p.

Selected work list, good discography. Includes brief but informative biographical profile.

B201. Viinholt Nielsen, Bendt. *Rued Langgaards Kompositioner; Annoteret værkfortegnelse.* Odense: Odense Universitetsforlag, 1991. 561 p.

Exhaustive annotated catalogue of the works of Rued Langgaard in Danish with an English introduction. Includes biography, numerous facsimiles of manuscripts and extensive bibliography.

B202. Viinholt Nielsen, Bendt. *The Compositions of Rued Langgaard (1893-1952): A Selective and Temporary List Including a Discography.* 1st ed. Copenhagen: MIC, 1984. 24 p.

B203. Widding, Kirsten. *Holmboes a cappella kormusik.* Copenhagen: Musikvidenskabeligt Institut Ved Københavns Universitet, 1975.

Discographies

B204. Balzer, Jurgen. *Catalogue of Danish music on records. Edited by Skandinavisk grammaphon aktieselskab in connection with the musical festival of the International Society for Contemporary Music, Copenhagen, May 29th to June 4th, 1947.* Copenhagen: Skandinavisk grammophon aktieselskab, 1947. 43 p.

In addition to the discography it includes a short survey of Danish musical history (pp. 3-8) and biographical sketches of three contemporary Danish composers (pp. 9-18) by J. Balzer.

B205. Bjørnum, Birgit. *Per Nørgårds kompositioner 1949-82.* Copenhagen: Edition Wilhelm Hansen, 1982.

See B164.

B206. "Danish Recordings 1988." *Musical Denmark.* 1 (1989): 17-24.

A list of recordings within all genres produced in Denmark, issued 1988 and containing Danish music or important Danish recordings of foreign music.

B207. *Danske grammofonplader.* Copenhagen: Nationaldiskoteket, 1969-.

An annually updated catalogue of Danish recordings by genre, with artist indexes.

B208. Dirckinck-Holmfeld, Gregers. "Ny dansk musik på lp-inspilninger." *Nutida Musik.* 5 (1962/63): 44-46.

List of Danish music recordings on lp.

B209. "Finn Saverys værkliste." *dmt.* 55: 1 (Sept. 1980): 22-23.

See B175.

B210. Hansen, Ivan. "Ny dansk musik på plade 1960-1980." *dmt.* No. 55:5 (April 1981): 253-57.

Discography of contemporary Danish music recorded during the period 1960-1980.

B211. Jensen, Jørgen I. *Bo Holten.* Copenhagen: Edition Wilhelm Hansen, c.1993. 8 p.

See B184.

B212. Johansen, Svend Aaquist. *Ib Nørholm.* Trans. Wayne Siegel. Copenhagen: Edition Wilhelm Hansen, 1985. 7 p.

See B185.

B213. Larsen, Freddy. *Dansk musik på plade.* Ballerup: Bibliotekscentralen, 1978. 83 p.

B214. Liliedahl, Karleric. *His Master's Voice: elektriska inspelningar i Skandinavien och for den skandinaviska marknaden, 1925-1934.* Stockholm: Arkivet for ljud och bild, 1990. 304 p.

Discography of lps produced by HMV for the Scandinavian market from 1925-34. Includes some works by Danish composers.

B215. *Music from Scandinavia.* Copenhagen: Nordic Council of Ministers, 1982. 179 p.

B216. *Musikplader og bånd, 1980 -.* Ballerup: Bibliotekscentralens Forlag, 1981-.

"Annual catalog of discs and cassettes offered by the Danish Library Bureau (Bibliotekscentralen) to Danish public libraries. Classified with indexes of titles, authors, composers, and performers."[10]

B217. Rasmussen, Karl Aage. *Per Nørgård.* Trans. Rosalind Bevan. Copenhagen: Edition Wilhelm Hansen, 1991. 10 p.

See B200.

B218. Rapoport, Paul. *Vagn Holmboe: A Catalog of Works and Recordings with Indexes of Persons and Titles.* 3rd ed. Copenhagen: Edition Wilhelm Hansen, 1996. 224 p.

See B198.

B219. Rosenberg, Herbert. "Danish music and musicians on record." *Musical Denmark.* 32 (1980/81): 14-18.

B220. Rosenberg, Herbert, ed. *Edition Balzer: a Danish History of Music in Sound.* Copenhagen: Nationaldiskoteket, 1966. 12 p.

Selective list of 53 recordings, with dates, matrix numbers, notes, and composer index, compiled by the author from the archives of Skandinavisk Grammophon Aktieselskab.

Journals and Periodicals

B221. *Ascolta.* Ed. Jørgen Krisand. Vaerløse: Operaens Venner.

Bi-monthly publication on opera premieres, news, recordings, performers and composers in Denmark.

B222. *Ballade, Tidsskrift for Ny Musik.* Ed. Geir Johnson. Oslo: Universitetsforlaget A/S.

Scholarly journal of contemporary music in Norway. Occasional articles on Danish music and composers. In Norwegian.

B223. *Bulletin.* Copenhagen: Samfundet til udgivelse af dansk musik.

News bulletin of SAMFUNDET. Occasional articles on musical life.

B224. *Cæcilia.* Århus: Musikvidenskabeligt Institut ved Århus Universitet.

Yearly publication by the Musicology Dept. at Århus University. In Danish.

B225. *Dansk Aarbog for Musikforskning.* Ed. Bo Merschner and Finn Egeland Hansen. Copenhagen: Dansk Selskab for Musikforskning.

Yearbook of musicology. In Danish. Published annually.

B226. *Dansk Musik Årbog.*

See B182.

B227. *Dansk musiker tidende.* Copenhagen: Dansk Musiker Forbund.

"Articles about musical events, performances in Denmark and other countries. Lists of new published music and books, discographies."[11]

B228. *dmt (Dansk Musiktidsskrift).* Ed. Anders Beyer. Copenhagen: Foreningen Dansk Musikstidsskrift.

Excellent scholarly journal with articles, analyses, interviews, reviews, reports, biographies. Focuses on contemporary art-music in Denmark. 8 times/yr.

B229. *Electronic Music and Musical Acoustics.* Ed. Finn Egeland Hansen. Aarhus: Department of Musical Acoustics, The Institute of Musicology, University of Aarhus.

Scholarly and often highly technical journal of analyses of works (both acoustic and electronic) and topics pertaining to the generation of electronic music and actual hardware and software. Published annually from 1975-77.

B230. *Information om Nordisk Musikforskning.* Copenhagen: Musikvidenskabeligt Institut Ved Københavns Universitet.

Journal about current musicology in Scandinavia. Primarily earlier time periods, but some contemporary issues. Published irregularly.

B231. *Kvinder i Musik.* Ed. Inge Bruland. Copenhagen: Foreningen Kvinder i Musik.

Journal covering women composers, performers, and issues concerning the role of women in Danish and Scandinavian musical life. Quarterly.

B232. *Levende musik.* Copenhagen: Dansk Musikpædagogisk Forening (The Danish Music Teacher's Association).

Published from 1942-47, *Levende musik* was the primary channel for information concerning The Danish Music Teacher's Association. Also included articles on contemporary Danish music, composers and musical life.

B233. *Libretto.* Copenhagen: Dansk Musikbiblioteks Forening (Danish Music Librarians' Association).

The Journal for Music Libraries (in Danish). *Libretto* is distributed freely to the members of the association, and deals broadly with musical topics with the focus on music documentation. Quarterly.

B234. *Modus.* Copenhagen: Dansk Musikpædagogisk Forening (The Danish Music Teacher's Association).

Primarily a news bulletin for The Danish Music Teacher's Association.

B235. *Musical Denmark.* Ed. Bendt Viinholt Nielsen. Copenhagen: Det Danske Kulturinstitut/MIC.

Non-scholarly periodical covering current musical events and performances, reviews, interviews, new releases. In English. Irregular.

B236. *Musical Denmark Yearbook.* Copenhagen: Danish Cultural Institute/MIC.

B237. *Musik & forskning.* Ed. Jan Maegaard. Copenhagen: Musikvidenskabeligt Institut, Københavns Universitet.

Yearbook for research and musicology in Denmark. Primarily earlier time periods, but also covers contemporary composers and issues. Annual.

B238. *Musikeren.* Ed. Henrik Strube. Copenhagen: Dansk Musiker Forbund.

Monthly periodical published by the Danish Musicians Union covering various aspects of musical life. Occasional articles on contemporary music and/or composers.

B239. *Musikrevy.* Ed. Bengt Pleijel. Stockholm: Nordisk Tidskrift För Musik och Grammofon.

Current musical events and performances, reviews, interviews, new releases. Occasional articles pertaining to Danish music or composers. 8 times/year.

B240. *MusikTexte; Zeitschrift für neue Musik*. Ed. Gisela Gronemeyre and Reinhard Oehlschlägel. Cologne: Falkenstein & Kirsten.

Journal of contemporary music in Germany. Frequently covers composers and musical events in Scandinavia and other Northern European countries. In German. 5 times/yr.

B241. *Nordic Sounds*. Ed. Anders Beyer. Copenhagen: NOMUS, Nordic Council of Ministers.

Non-scholarly overview of current musical events in Scandinavia. Quarterly.

B242. *Nordisk Musikkultur*. Ed. Sigurd Berg. Copenhagen: Nordisk Kulturministeriet/Secretariat for Nordic Cultural Cooperation

Nordisk Musikkultur was an effort to produce a scholarly journal that covered all aspects of musical life in Scandinavia. Published quarterly from 1952-58 as a joint publication with with *dmt* and *Nutida Musik*, then as a separate journal focusing primarily on Norwegian music until 1963.

B243. *Norsk Musikerblad*. Ed. Tore Nordvik. Oslo: Norsk Musikerforbund.

Current musical events and performances, reviews, interviews, new releases. Occasional articles on Danish musical life and composers. Monthly.

B244. *Nutida Musik*. Ed. Bo Rydberg. Stockholm: Svenska Sektionen av ISCM/Statens Kulturråd.

Scholarly journal of contemporary music in Sweden. Frequent articles on Danish music. Quarterly.

B245. *P2-Musik*. Ed. Bette Thomas. Copenhagen: Danmarks Radio.

Publication by Danmarks Radio with program guide and brief articles about upcoming broadcasts on P2 including the weekly show of contemporary music, "Lyt til Nyt."

B246. *Tværstand*. Ed. Lars Grunth. Copenhagen: Statens Musikråd.

General coverage of musical life and issues in Denmark. Occasional articles on contemporary composers. Quarterly.

Articles from Journals and Periodicals

Note: All articles are in the same language as the title unless otherwise indicated.

B247. Anderberg, Thomas. "Rued Langgaard - en förtidig modernist och försenad romantiker." *Artes: Kvartalskrift for litteratur, konst och musik*. 6 (1984): 26-31.

B248. Andersen, Mogens. "Gunnar Berg og hans galiciske triptyk." *Nutida Musik*. 5 (1962/63): 18-23.

Analysis of Berg's *Galicisk triptyk* ('57). Musical examples. Brief bio and illustration by the composer.

B249. Andersen, Mogens. "Dag-mareridt og Moraliteter - en introduktion til Ib Nørholms symfonier (3)." *dmt* 5 (1985/86): 224-232.

Part three of an excellent, in-depth series of articles on the background and analyses of the symphonies of Ib Nørholm. Focus on symphonies no. 3 and 6. Extensive musical examples.

B250. Andersen, Mogens. "Isola Bella genoplevet - en introduktion til Ib Nørholms symfonier (1)." *dmt*. 5/6 (1984/85): 314-335.

Part one of the above listed series. Focus on 2nd symphony. Extensive musical examples.

B251. Andersen, Mogens. "Modskabelse - en introduktion til Ib Nørholms symfonier (2)." *dmt*. 2 (1985/86): 60-68.

Part three of the above listed series. Focus on 4th symphony.
Extensive musical examples.

B252. Andersen, Mogens. "Tonaliteter. Om struktur og betydning i Ib
Nørholms symfonier og om tonalitet som fænomen og begreb."
Dansk Årbog for Musikforskning 1995. XXIII (1996): 39-62.

Informative and insightful overview of the symphonies of Ib
Nørholm, with a focus on form, structure, and tonality. Charts,
musical examples, bibliography.

B253. Andersen, Mogens. "Vagn Holmboes Epitaph." *Nutida musik.* 3:6
(1959/60): 6-8.

B254. Balzer, Jürgen. "Knudåge Riisager: *Qarrtsiluni.*" *Levende musik.*
(1942): 26-29.

B255. Balzer, Jürgen. "Vagn Holmboe: Portrait of a Composer." *Musical
Denmark.* 21 (1969/70): 4-7.

B256. Beckman, Jesper. "Gennem århundreders tårer: en samtale med
komponisten Poul Ruders." *dmt.* 6 (1985/86): 248-57.

Interview and profile of the composer. Includes work list and
musical examples.

B257. Bentzon, Niels Viggo. "Forsøg på status." *Nutida Musik.* 3 (1954):
79-82.

Brief but insightful essay on issues and problems facing modern
composers in the context of expectations and relationships resulting
from "traditional" art-music from Palestrina through the 19th
century.

B258. Bentzon, Niels Viggo. "Tradition og fornyelse - Tre værker af
Herman D. Koppel: *Klaverkoncert nr 3, strygekvartet nr 3* og *Tre
Davidssalmer* for tenor-solo, blandet kor, drengekor og orkester."
Nordisk Musikkultur. (1952): 267-70.

B259. Bentzon, Niels Viggo and Frede Schandorf Petersen. "Hvad har
gyldighed?" *dmt.* 1 (1952): 198-201.

Interesting dialog discussing the various trends in new music both in
and outside of Denmark, foreign perceptions of Danish music, the

value and validity of various movements & theories, and the perception of the "absolute" vs. the "relative."

B260. Bergendal, Göran, ed. "Norden nu!" *Nutida Musik.* 4 (1972/73): 1+.

Special theme issue of *Nutida Musik* coinciding with the Norden nu festival (Copenhagen, 5/29-31, 1973). Several informative articles on Danish composers and musical life. Includes interviews with Ib Nørholm, Pelle Gudmundsen-Holmgreen, and Per Nørgård, and articles on Jørgen Plætner and the electronic music studio in Holstebro, and the Danish new music organization Gruppen for Alternativ Musik.

B261. Bergendal, Göran. "Orfeus och Atlantis." *Nutida Musik.* 3 (1972/73): 60-62.

Interview with the Danish composer Ingolf Gabold, with a focus on his opera *Syv scener til Orfeus.*

B262. Beyer, Anders. "An established outsider in contemporary Danish music: an interview with Pelle Gudmundsen-Holmgreen." *Ballade, Tidsskrift for Ny Musik.* 16: 3 (1992): 74-78.

B263. Beyer, Anders. "Balancen mellem emotionerne og fornuften." *dmt.* 7 (1989/90):

Interview with composer Vagn Holmboe. Includes list of works composed since the first edition of Paul Rapoport's biography and catalogue in 1979.

B264. Beyer, Anders. "Between Heaven and Hell. Bent Sørensen, Winner of the Nordic Council's Music Prize 1996." *Nordic Sounds.* 4 (1995): 3-6.

Portrait of the composer, who won the 1996 Nordic Council's Music Prize for the violin concerto *Sterbende Garten.*

B265. Beyer, Anders. "Choral music of international standard: a portrait of the Ars Nova choir." *Musical Denmark.* 39 (1988): 9-12.

B266. Beyer, Anders. "Dansk musik i Øst og Vest." *dmt.* 5 (Jan./Feb. 1993/94): 165-7.

Discusses the exchange of contemporary music between Denmark and Russia, as well as the Center for the Study of Danish Music at the University of Louisville, KY.

B267.   Beyer, Anders. "In Search of the Ultimate Simplification. A Portrait of Danish Composer Leif Thybo." *Nordic Sounds.* 2 (1994): 19-22.

Very informative introduction to the often overlooked composer Thybo. Selective list of works.

B268.   Beyer, Anders. "Om Per Nørgård's 5. Symfoni." *dmt.* 3 (1990/91): 75-81.

Interview with Per Nørgård and analysis of his 5th symphony. Many musical examples.

B269.   Beyer, Anders. "Skygge eller skikkelse: Billederne bagved." *dmt.* 5 (Feb. 1991/92): 146-153.

Interview with composer Bent Sørensen. Includes musical examples and list of works.

B270.   Bisgaard, Lars. "Musikalsk hermeneutik på hierarkisk grundlag: Bidrag til en musikalsk fænomenologi. I." *Dansk Årbog for Musikforskning.* 16 (1985).

Part one of an in-depth discussion of the "cyclical-hierarchical method of musical analysis developed by the author and based on the hierarchical theory of music of the Danish composer Per Nørgård...and the mapping of the human unconscious carried out by the Czech-American psychologist Stanislav Grof." Includes musical examples and bibliography.

B271.   Bisgaard, Lars. "Musikalsk hermeneutik på hierarkisk grundlag: Bidrag til en musikalsk fænomenologi. II." *Dansk Årbog for Musikforskning.* (1986): 69-92.

Part two of the above article.

B272.   Bisgaard, Lars. "Per Nørgårds 2. *Symfoni*: en rejsebeskrivelse." *dmt.* 2 (Nov. 1974): 57-61.

Part one of a detailed discussion of Nørgård's *Symphony No. 2*, with an analysis of the use of infinity series. Includes graphs and musical examples.

B273. Bisgaard, Lars. "Per Nørgårds *2. Symfoni*: en rejsebeskrivelse II." *dmt.* 3 (Dec. 1974): 28-31.

Part two of the above listed article.

B274. Blak, Kristian. "Musical Renaissance in the North Atlantic." *dmt.* 1 (1994/95): 22-25.

Discussion of the history and development of contemporary music in the Faroe Islands, with brief bios of important emerging composers.

B275. Boehm, G. "Kopenhagen: Wo die Uhren anders gehen." *Buehne: das Österreichische Kulturmagazin.* (Dec. 1985): 41-43.

Review of Kundåge Riisager's ballet *Mascarade*.

B276. Brahm, Erling. "Oluf Ring og det folkelige Musikarbejde." *Dansk Udsyn.* (1946): 314-29.

B277. Bray, David. "Poul Ruders: 'a film-composer with no film:' the Danish composer." *Musical Times.* 131 (Sept. 1990): 479-81.

Portrait of the composer.

B278. Brincker, Jens. "Brev til en ukendt adressat om en afdød komponist." *dmt.* 3 (Nov. 1992/93): 84-91.

A tribute to composer Poul Rovsing Olsen commemorating ten years since his death. Includes list of works.

B279. Brincker, Jens. "Interview med fire komponister." *Nutida Musik.* 7 (1964/65): 205-210.

Interesting interview with five - not four, as the title implies - Danish composers: Per Nørgård and four of his then students at the Royal Danish Conservatory of Music - Erik Norby, Svend Nielsen, Ingolf Gabold and Jens Wilhelm Pedersen (aka "Fuzzy").

B280. Brincker, Jens. "Nye strömningar i 1970'erne. Hvad dom ud af kulturoptimism i 1960'erne?" *Nutida Musik.* 3 (19080/81): 15-17.

Follows the work of several of Per Nørgård's students who left the
Royal Danish Conservatory of Music in 1965 in protest over the
conservatism at the institution and moved to the Royal Academy of
Music in Aarhus.

B281. Brincker, Jens. "Three Modern Nordic Composers." *Nordic
Sounds.* 1 (1982): 22-26.

Brief portraits of the Norwegian Arne Nordheim, the Swede Ingvar
Lidholm, and Per Nørgård.   Selective work list.

B282. Brulund, Inge. "Fire danske kvindelige komponister fra det 20.
århundrede." *Årbog for kvindeforskning.* 5 (1986): 33-59.

Portraits of four Danish women composers: Else Marie Pade,
Gudrun Lund, Diana Pereira and Birgitte Alsted.

B283. Brulund, Inge. "Kvinden og klaveret: København 1900-1950."
Musik & forskning. 20 (1994/95): 81-100.

Discussion of the various roles which women pianists played in the
music scene in Copenhagen in the first half of the 20th century.
Focus is on popular music genre, and obsticles presented by the
traditional gender roles in professional concert life. Brief discussion
of the women pianist/composers Benna Moe, Else Printz and
Margaret Williams.

B284. Brulund, Inge. "Profiler." *dmt.* 4 (Dec. 1992/93): 110-121.

Brief profiles of several Danish women composers, with a focus on
Else Marie Pade and Birgitte Alsted.   Photos, selective work lists.

B285. Bucht, Gunnar. "Skandinavien; eine musikalische Einheit?" *The
world of music/Die Welt der Musik/Le monde de la musique,
International.* 11.2 (1969): 18-31.

An evaluation of the stylistic unity of contemporary music in
Scandinavia.   Discusses influences and trends in the late 1960's. In
English, French and German.

B286. Bønnerup, Inge. "Orgelmusik af Vagn Holmboe." *Organist-Bladet.*
43:8 (August 1977): 265-75.

B287. Caron, Jean-Luc. "A la découverte de Rued Langgaard." *Bulletin de l'association française Carl Nielsen.* 3, 1 (1987): 27-95.

B288. Carritt, Graham. "Vagn Holmboe." *Anglo Dania.* 27, no.5 (Nov. 1958): 26-28.

B289. Carritt, Graham. "Vagn Holmboe: a modern Danish composer." *The Listener.* 59, no. 1502 (Jan. 9, 1958): 81.

B290. Chestnut, Michael. "Cantio sacra: The Music of Bernhard Lewkovitch." *Nordic Sounds.* (Dec. 1987): 2-5.

B291. Christensen, Erik. "Talløse varianter mellem det enkle og det komplicerede." *dmt.* 1 (Sept. 1980): 15-21.

Profile of the composer Finn Savery.

B292. Christensen, Erik. "Zwischen Chaos und Ordnung. Per Nørgård im Gespräch." *MusikTexte.* 50 (Aug. 1993).

Interview with Per Nørgård.

B293. Christensen, Jean. "Heroes of the Inner Universe: The Operas of Per Nørgård." *The Opera Journal.* 28, 4 (1995): 2-10.

B294. Christensen, Jean. "Lyt Dansk - Den danske klang: Komponistforeningens 75-Års jubilæumsmusikdage." *dmt.* 63, 4 (1988/89): 119-120.

B295. Christensen, Jean. "Nørgård: *Siddharta.*" *The Opera Journal.* 29, 1 (1996): 61-64.

B296. Christensen, Jean. "Per Nørgård: Widening the Framework." *Musical Denmark.* 1 (1989): 3-5.

Brief biography on Per Nørgård, tracing his stylistic path from the 1960's to the present.

B297. Christensen, Jean. "Per Nørgårds 3. Symfoni." *Ballade, Tidsskrift for Ny Musik.* II, 3 (1978): 20-25.

B298. Christensen, Jean. "Per Nørgård's works for early music ensemble." *Journal of the Viola da Gamba Society of America.* 22 (1985):35-41.

Discussion and brief analyses of Nørgård's works written for the

Danish early music ensemble Sub Rosa: *Nova Genitura* and *Seadrift*. Musical examples.

B299. Christensen, Jean. "Play on!" *Nordic Sounds*. 3 (1994): 24-25.

B300. Christensen, Severin. "Rud Langgaards symfoniske Værker." *Musik*. (1918): 57-60.

B301. Christiansen, Anna Sofie, and Brad Garton, Mara Helmuth. "Three Reviews of the 1994 International Computer Music Conference." *Computer Music Journal*. 19, 2 (Summer, 1995): 97-102.

Review of the ICMC festival held at DIEM (Danish Institute for Electroacoustic Music) in Aarhus, Sept. 12-17, 1994.

B302. Christiansen, John. "Aarhus - City of Contemporary Music." *Musical Opinion*. (July 1981): 383-384.

Discusses current state of modern music in Aarhus, Denmark's second largest city. Lists ensembles, orchestras, conservatories, composers, etc.

B303. Cockshott, G. "Knudåge Riisager." *Music in Education*. 30 (1966): 237.

Brief profile of the composer, with an emphasis on his pedagogical role in Danish musical life.

B304. Colding-Jorgensen, Gunnar. "Den unge Rued Langgaard og Carl Nielsen." *dmt*. (1968): 190-92.

A look at the two composers and the æsthetic disagreement in Danish musical life during the first half of the century.

B305. Crome, Fritz. "Peder Gram." *Musik*. (1921): 143-47.

B306. Damm, A. "10. NUMUS festival in Aarhus." *Musik und Gesellschaft*. (July 1988): 380.

B307. Debièvre, Pierre. "Un grand compositeur danois." *La vie musicale*. (Dec. 1959): 114.

Profile of Knudåge Riisager. Selective work list.

B308. *dmt.* 43, 7-8 (1968): 1+.

Special theme issue on Rued Langgaard with contributions by Bo
Wallner, Tage Nielsen, Jens Brincker and Gunnar Colding-
Jørgensen.

B309. Dirckinck-Holmfeld, Gregers. "Kald mig bare eksistentialist."
Nutida Musik. 5 (1962/63): 49-50.

Interview with Niels Viggo Bentzon.

B310. Dirckinck-Holmfeld, Gregers. "Seks unge." *Nutida Musik.* 5
(1962/63): 31-37.

Portraits and selective work lists of six "young" composers: Henning
Christiansen, Pelle Gudmundsen-Holmgreen, Mogens Winkel-Holm,
Ib Nørholm, Jørgen Plætner and Finn Savery. Photos.

B311. Dørge, Pierre. "En lang, frugtbar rejse." *Tværstand.* 26 (1996).

The director of the New Jungle Orchestra discusses their three-year
tenure (1993-96) as the official state music ensemble.

B312. Eisler, Hanns. "Musikalsk realisme: Brev til Vesttyskland." *Dialog.*
2, 4 (July 1952): 18-23.

Discussion of the "crisis in music and musical life" faced by
composers. Of particular interest in that it spurred a response by the
Danish composer Finn Høffding. *See also* B352.

B313. "Enquéte: Nordisk sind - nonsens?" *Nutida Musik.* 4 (1956): 105-9.

In response to Per Nørgård's article urging increased cooperation
and interaction between Scandinavian composers, four composers
reply: Klaus Egge (Nor), Karl-Birger Blomdahl (S), Kjell
Bækkelund (Nor), and Niels Viggo Bentzon (DK). *See also* B439
and B442.

B314. Fallentin, Niels Hoff. "Erindringer om Rued Langgaard." *Dansk
Kirkemusiker Tidende.* 2 (March 1972): 14-16.

B315. Fanger, Eva-Britt. "The Danish National Bibliography of Music:
Problems Connected with its Establishment." *Fontes artis musicae.*
27:2 (April-July 1980): 67-70.

Discusses the problems encountered while compiling *Dansk musikfortegnelse* (*see* B171).

B316. "First Performances 1987." *Musical Denmark.* 1 (1989): 15-16.

A list of premiere performances of Danish works in the field of light orchestral music, big band, experimental jazz and related popular genres, as reported to the Danish Music Information Centre.

B317. Fjeldsøe, Michael. "En nordisk naturlyriker: et portræt af komponisten Sunleif Rasmussen." *dmt.* 7 (May/June 1993/94): 234-239.

Portrait of Faroese composer Sunleif Rasmussen. Includes list of works.

B318. Fjeldsøe, Michael. "Metamorphosen. Vagn Holmboe, 1909-1996." *MusikTexte.* 66 (Nov. 1996): 66-67.

A tribute to the life and work of Holmboe upon his death.

B319. Frank, Tine. "Rued Langgaard: A Symbolistic Composer?" *Dansk Årbog for Musikforskning.* XXIII (1995): 31-37.

Discusses the connections of Langgaard's music to the *fin-de-siècle* atmosphere and symbolistic movements in art and poetry in Denmark around the turn of the century.

B320. Frederiksen, Steen. "Mladá dánská hudba." *Opus musicum, Czechoslovakia.* (1969): 207-09.

Summarizes currents of contemporary Danish music after Carl Nielsen; includes information on several individual composers. In Czech.

B321. Frounberg, Ivar. "Darmstadt og Danmark: Hvad er pære og hvad er vælling?" *dmt.* (1981/82): 226-29.

B322. Frounberg, Ivar. "Vedr. Per Nørgårds 'Henimod en optimalt økonomisk signalsytematik,' med svar fra Per Nørgård og Jesper Beckman." *dmt.* (1987/88): 177-179.

A discussion of Per Nørgård's "Hierarchic Genesis; Steps Towards a Natural Musical Theory" (translation found in *Dansk Aarbog for*

Musikforskning. XIV, 1983). In debate form between Per Nørgård and Jesper Beckman, another Danish composer and theorist.

B323. Fundal, Karsten. "Den stilfærdige revolution." *dmt.* 6 (April 1993/94): 192-93.
Discusses the musical mileu, challenges and possibilites facing young composers in Denmark today.

B324. Gefors, Hans. "En Skiss af *Innehaalet* i Per Nørgårds musik." *Nutida Musik.* 2 (1978/79): 68-69.

An examination of Nørgård's *Third Symphony*, with a focus on the "hierarchical" relationships in the form and music. Musical examples.

B325. Goldbæk, Henning. "En forunderlig musikhistorie: et interview med komponisten Bent Lorentzen." *dmt.* 1 (1990/91): 3-9.

Interview with composer Bent Lorentzen. Includes list of works.

B326. Gudmundsen-Holmgreen, Pelle. "Nyenkelhet ännu en gång." *Nutida Musik.* 22: 3/4 (1978/79): 31-36.

The composer discusses the "New Simplicity" movement and the reasons for its development, with a focus on the Danish composers active in the style during the 1960's.

B327. Gudmundsen-Holmgreen , Pelle. "Stemmen i dansk musik." *Nutida Musik.* 21:3 (1977/78): 55.

Brief discussion of current trends in Danish music.

B328. Guldbrandsen, Erling E. "Om Per Nørgård, Kronoskvartetten og dansk jovialitet: rapport fra NUMUS-festivalen." *Ballade, Tidsskrift for Ny Musik.* 11:2 (1987): 17+.

B329. Hambræus, Bengt. "En hel klodes musikalske erfaringer." *Nutida Musik.* 5 (1962/63): 50-52.

Interview with Poul Rovsing Olsen.

B330. Hansen, Finn Egeland. "Just Intonation in the Renaissance and in the Music of Per Nørgård." *Electronic Music and Musical Acoustics.* 3 (1977): 49-58.

Discussion of the development of various tuning systems in the Renaissance and a just intonation tuning system developed by Per Nørgård.

B331. Hansen, Finn Egeland. "Per Nørgård's *Canon* for Organ." *Electronic Music and Musical Acoustics.* 2 (1976): 43-99.

Detailed, technical analysis of Nørgård's *Canon*, with an emphasis on use of the Fibonacci series and the infinity row. Numerous charts and musical examples.

B332. Hansen, Finn Egeland. "Rapport fra 9. Nordiske Musikforsker-møde." *Dansk Aarbog for Musikforskning.* 14 (1983): 5-16.

Report and program from the 9th annual Convention of Scandinavian Musicology.

B333. Hansen, Ivan. "Percussion in Denmark." *Musical Denmark.* 1 (1989): 6-11.

Overview of Danish percussion ensembles and recent works for percussion by Danish composers.

B334. Hansen, Ivan. "Slagtøj og ny musik; Gert Mortensen i samtale." *dmt.* 6 (1982/83): 271-79.

Interview with percussionist Gert Mortensen regarding contemporary percussion music. Includes list of recordings of Danish works for solo percussion, percussion ensembles and chamber works.

B335. Haumann, Erik. "*Messis* - en analyse." *Organistbladet.* 51.3 (March 1985): 83-103.

Analysis of Rued Langgaard's *Messis*. Musical examples.

B336. "Henning Christiansen portræt." *dmt.* 4 (1986/87): 172-205.

A series of four articles and a lengthy interview with the experimental composer Henning Christiansen. Some focus on his opera *Penthesilea.* Many photos, musical examples.

B337. Hetsch, Gustav. "Knudåge Riisager." *Musikjounalen.* (Sept. - Oct. 1947): 12-16.

B338. Hedelund, Ivo. "Skitse af en ny dansk tonekunstnergeneration." *Nutida Musik.* 27.3 (1983/84): 15-19.

B339. Hinman, Clifford. "Om Svend S. Schultz." *Musikvärlden.* (1946): 34-36.

B340. Holm, Mogens Winkel. "Hvordan går det med kompositions-musikken?" *Dansk Musik Årbog 1991.* 1991: 104-105.

Brief article on the progress of DKF (The Danish Composers Society) and its role in Danish musical life.

B341. Holm, Sven. "Fanfare for a Danish Outsider." *Nordic Sounds.* 3 (1993): 3-8.

Good introduction to the composer Rued Langgaard. Emphasis on recent recording and publications. Selective discography.

B342. Holmboe, Vagn. "Herman D. Koppel." *Aarstiderne.* (1942-43): 72-75.

B343. Holmboe, Vagn. "Lidt om moderne musik." *dmt.* 1 (Jan. 1936): 21-24.

B344. Holmboe, Vagn. "Strejflys over nogle problemer i dansk musik." *Prisma.* 2 (1950): 57-61.

Excellent article discussing various aspects of musical life and stylistic problems faced by Danish composers in the 1940's. Special focus on the debate on the existence and definition of a "national art." Discusses works by Jørgen Bentzon, Niels Viggo Bentzon, Hamerik, Høffding, Koppel, Riisager, Schultz, Tarp and Weis.

B345. Holten, Bo and Kaare Hansen. "*Rejsen inde i den Gyldne Skærm.* En analyse af Per Nørgårds værk i to satser for kammerorkester." *dmt.* 10 (1971): 232-36.

Detailed analysis of *Rejsen inde i den Gyldne Skærm* for chamber orchestra, the first major work based on the infinity series. Musical examples.

B346. Holten, Bo. "Vagn Holmboe i dag." *dmt.* 4 (June 1977): 140-144.

Interesting interview with the composer, discussing his own style and ideas, as well as his thoughts on many other composers, past and present. Includes list of works.

B347. Hove, Richard. "Dansk musik i dag." *Tidsskrift for dansk Folkeopolysning.* (1930): 65-81.

Summary of current movements in Danish musical life. Brief commentary on some prominent composers.

B348. Hove, Richard. "Försög på en musikalsk status." *Nordisk tidskrift för vetenskap, konst och industri.* 24, 7-8 (1948): 382-91.

Overview of the major compositional figures - outside of Carl Nielsen - in Denmark in the late 19th century and first half of the 20th century.

B349. Hove, Richard. "Tre nordiske Symfonikere." *Nordisk Tidsskrift.* (1936): 571-89.

Portraits of three Scandinavian symphonic composers: Hilding Rosenberg, Harald Sæverud, and Finn Høffding. Selective work lists.

B350. "Hvad er moderne Opera?" *Pro cantu.* (1942): 3-4.

Interview with Finn Høffding, with a focus on contemporary opera.

B351. "Hvad siger kollegerne?" *dmt.* 5-6 (1952):198-201.

The leading composers of the day share their feelings about Stravinsky. Provides interesting insight into how Stravinsky was perceived in Danish musical culture and the influence he had on Danish composers. Contributors include Finn Høffding, Svend Erik Tarp, Herman D. Koppel, Vagn Holmboe, Jorgen Jersild, Niels Viggo Bentzon, Svend Westergaard, Bernhard Lewkovitch, and Svend S. Schultz.

B352. Høffding, Finn. "Musikalsk realisme." *Dialog.* 2, 7 (Dec. 1952): 30-32.

Discusses the relevance of "new-music" in a political/social context, responding to an article by Hanns Eisler (*see* B312).

B353. Jacoby, Jan. "Finn Høffding - Music as a Humanistic Way of Life." *Nordic Sounds.* 2 (1984): 14-16.

Portrait of the composer. Selective work list.

B354. Jensen, Jørgen I. "Alle tings musik: At lytte til Rued Langgaard - og særlig til hans opera *Antikrist.*" *dmt.* 6 (May 1980): 273-294.

B355. Jensen, Jørgen I. "At the Boundry between Music and Science: From Per Nørgård to Carl Nielsen." *Fontes Artis Musicae.* 42/1 (Jan.-March, 1995): 55-61.

Brief yet interesting discussion of the influence of the mathematical and natural sciences on the music and theories of Per Nørgård, in particular fractals, chaos theory and the Golden Section.

B356. Jensen, Jørgen I. "En symfoni om en novelle." *dmt.* 2 (Nov. 1979): 78-83.

Commentary and analysis of Bo Holten's opera *The Bond*, based on the novel *The Ring* by Karen Blixen.

B357. Jensen, Jørgen I. "Hans Abrahamsen, Per Nørgård og ny dansk musik." *Nutida Musik.* 30.1 (1986/87): 12-20.

B358. Jensen, Jørgen I. "Skjulte dagsordener: Nye udfordringer - og naboer - i Per Nørgård's musik." *dmt.* 8 (June/July 1991/92): 254-264.

In-depth discussion of the late works of Per Nørgård, with numerous music examples.

B359. Jensen, Jørgen I. "Tide og utide: Omkring Karl Aage Rasmussens tids-symfoni." *dmt.* 5/6 (1984/85): 262-72.

B360. Jensen, Niels Martin. "Saa sagte fin en sommerklang. En introduktion til Rued Langgaards sange med klaver." *Musik.* 3 (1969/70): 15-17.

Brief overview of Langgaard's songs for voice and piano. Selected work list.

B361. Jerrild, Holger. "Hos Dr. Knud Jeppesen." *Gads dansk Magasin.* (1943): 173-80.

B362. Jersild, Jørgen. "Rytmisk kompleksitet." *Nutida Musik.* 5 (1962/63): 38-41.

The composer discusses issues of rhythmic complexity, notation and modulation. Musical examples.

B363. Johannessen, Per Berge. "On the Infinity Series." *Electronic Music and Musical Acoustics.* 2 (1976): 101-108.

B364. Johnsson, Bengt. "Axel Borup-Jörgensen og hans *Cretaufoni.*" *Nutida Musik.* 5 (1962/63): 9-13.

Analysis of *Cretaufoni* (1960/61) for orchestra. Musical examples. Brief bio of composer. List of works.

B365. Johnsson, Bengt. "Contemporary Danish Piano Music." *Music Journal.* 23:4 (April 1965): 73-96 passim.

An overview of 20th century Danish piano repertoire and important composers of piano music, including Flemming Weis, Jørgen Jersild, Niels Viggo Bentzon, Poul Rovsing Olsen and Axel Borup Jørgensen.

B366. Johnsson, Bengt. "Lewkovitch og den nye kirkemusik." *Nutida Musik.* 5 (1962/63): 42-43.

Discusses the role of new sacred music in liturgical settings. Focuses on Bernhard Lewkovitch, for whom church music represents the bulk of his output.

B367. Johnsson, Bengt. "To danske klaverkomponister." *Norsk Musiktidsskrift.* 9:4 (Dec. 1972): 150-63.

Portraits of the composers Flemming Weis and Poul Rovsing Olsen, with special attention to their piano music. Musical examples, list of works. In German.

B368. Johnsson, Bengt. "Hvorledes man torturerer et geni." *dmt.* 57 (April 1982/83): 159-63.

B369. Jørgensen, Klaus Ib. "Moderne gennem 125 år, Samfundet til udgivelse af dansk musik." *Tværstand.* 27 (1996).

B370. Karlsson, E.M. "Imponerande samling kring datormusik i Aarhus." *Nutida Musik.* 3 (1992): 47.

Brief article on computer music at DIEM.

B371. Ketting, Knud. "Axel Borup-Jørgensen." *dmt.* 1 (Sept. 1977): 45-51.

Profile of the composer. Musical examples, comprehensive work list.

B372. Ketting, Knud. "Recorded Danish Music." *dmt.* Special Issue in English (1971): 133-36.

Overview of the prominent Danish classical record labels with a focus on the recording of contemporary Danish music.

B373. Ketting, Knud. "Two Ballets, Two Kinds of Music, One Composer." *Nordic Sounds.* (March 1989): 6-7.

Discussion of two recent ballets by the Faroese composer Kristian Blak: *The Four Towers* and *Harra Pætur og Elinborg*.

B374. Ketting, Knud. "When the paper begins to answer." *Nordic Sounds.* March 1986: 21-23.

Profile of the composer Erik Norby.

B375. Kjeldsen, Bente Honore. "Public Music Libraries in Denmark." *Fontes Artis Musicæ.* 34.2 (March 1987): 150+.

In English, French and German.

B376. Kjerulf, Axel. "Musiklivet i Danmark, 1914-35." *Danmark i Fest og Glæde.* VI (1936).

B377. Kock, Sven. "Niels Viggo Bentzon." *Pro cantu.* (1941): 38-39.

B378. Kragh-Jacobsen, Svend. "The Music of Denmark: A History of the Danish Ballet." *Music Journal.* 21: 3 (March 1963): 37-65 passim.

An historical survey of the Danish ballet. The only 20th century composer to receive any attention is Knudåge Riisager, with attention to his collaborations with the dramatic writer Kjeld Abell and his ballet *Qarrtsiluni*.

B379. Krarup, Bertel. "Franz Syberg: en outsider i dansk mellemkrigsmusik." *dmt.* 3 (1990/91): 88-94.

Profile of the composer Franz Syberg and analysis of *Symphony*. Includes musical examples and list of works.

B380. Krarup, Bertel. "LIN Ensemble: Ny musik så hatten passer." *dmt.* 6 (1990/91): 96-98.

Profile of the contemporary music ensemble LIN Ensemble.

B381. Krarup, Bertel. "Niels Viggo Bentzon og *Det Tempererede Klaver*." *dmt.* 2 (1990/91): 50-55.

Analysis of Bentzon's epic piano work with numerous musical examples.

B382. Krarup, Bertel. "Unge danske: Jesper Hendze: mellem slagtøg og computer." *dmt.* 4 (Dec. 1993/94) 125-131.

Portrait of composer Jesper Hendze. Includes list of works.

B383. Krisand, J. "Før *Dommen*." *Ascolta.* 2 (1996).

Interview with Kasper Holten and Steffen Aarfing about Niels Rosing-Schow's opera *Dommen*.

B384. Krumhardt, Anette. "Alting er opera. Skabelsen i musikken." *Flux.* 1 (1996).

Interview with Per Nørgård, part one.

B385. Krumhardt, Anette. "Fraktaler, tid og uendelig musik." *Flux.* 2 (1996).

Interview with Per Nørgård, part two.

B386. Kube, Michael. "Im Schatten der Musikgeschichte: Rued Langgaard (1893-1952)." *Norrøna.* 8, 16 (Oct. 1992): 35-39.

B387. Kullberg, Erling. "Da modernism kom til Danmark: samtale med Ib Nørholm om 60'ernes dansk musik og musikmiljø og om hans egen musik i særdeleshed." *dmt.* 60 (March 1985/86): 114-21.

Interview with In Nørholm focusing on the arrival of "modernism" in Denmark in the 60's, Danish musical life in the 60's and especially his own music.

B388. Kullberg, Erling. "Den hierarkiske musik. En introduktion til Per Nørgårds kompositionsteknik omkring midten af 70'erne." *dmt.* 3 (Dec. 1977): 97-105.

One of the definitive articles written on Nørgård's theories of hierarchic music, the infinity row, and use of the Golden Mean. Many charts and musical examples. Appears in a somewhat extended version in *Festskrift til Otto Mortensen på 70-årsdagen den 18. august 1977: fra kolleger og tidligere studerende ved Musikvidenskabeligt Institut, Aarhus Universitet* (*see* B72).

B389. Kullberg, Erling. "Hierarchic Music. On Per Nørgård's Latest Composition Technique Exemplified by an Analysis of the Choral Work *Frostsalme*." *Electronic Music and Musical Acoustics.* 3 (1977): 59-93.

A summary of the fundamental theory of hierarchic music and technical analysis of the three hierarchic "systems": the melodic infinity series, the rhythmic infinity system, and the harmonic infinity system. Lengthy, detailed analysis of Per Nørgård's *Frostsalme*, with numerous musical examples and diagrams.

B390. Kullberg, Erling. "Mellem dur og mol: INTERFERENS." *dmt.* 8 (June/July 1991/92): 266-273.

Analysis of Per Nørgård's *Night Symphonies, Day Breaks.* Many musical examples.

B391. Kullberg, Erling. "Ny enkelhed - på ny: Komponisten Ole Buck før og nu." *dmt.* 8 (June/July 1992/93): 270-275.

Profile of composer Ole Buck. Includes musical examples; no list of works.

B392. Langgaard, Rued. "Kunst og Salmesang." *Kirken.* 5 (1933): 68-72.

B393. Lasthein, Neils Martin. "Musical Life in Denmark." *Musical Opinion.* 102 (Feb. 1979): 221.

Very generalized and incomplete look at the current state of music in Denmark.

B394. Layton, Robert. "The Symphonies of Vagn Holmboe." *The Listener.* 73 (March 4, 1965): 349.

B395. Layton, Robert. "Vagn Holmboe: an Eightieth Birthday Salute." *Nordic Sounds.* Dec. 1989: 8-9.

Tribute to and portrait of the composer Vagn Holmboe.

B396. Lenz, Hansgeorg. "Det er ingen kvalitet i sig selv at være komponist." *dmt.* 5 (1986/87): 237-249.

Interview with composer Bernhard Lewkovitch. Includes musical examples and complete reprints of two short songs for tenor and piano; no list of works.

B397. Lesle, Lutz. "Göttin des Todes über Flandern. Per Nørgård im Gespräch." *Neue Zeitschrift für Musik.* 4 (1996): 47-49.

Portrait/interview with Per Nørgård, with an emphasis on the influence of Adolf Wölfi in his work. Brief discussion of *Nuit des Hommes* ('96). Selective discography.

B398. Lesle, Lutz. "Sonnenwahn, Himmelsriss und Donnerwohnung. Die Zeit des dänischen Komponisten Rued Langgaard ist gekommen." *Das Orchester; Zeitschrift fürOrchesterkultur.* 43, 9 (1995): 2-9.

B399. Lesle, Lutz. "Weltmusiktage de IGNM in Aarhus." *Das Orchester; Seitschrift für Orchesterkultur.* 32 (Feb. 1984): 117-19.

B400. Levinsen, Jakob. "Det' så udansk." *dmt.* 4 (Dec. 1992/93): 122-125.

Interview with composer/pop-singer Anne Linnet. Includes list of works.

B401. Lewkovitch, Bernhard. "Omkring en støvets sanger." *dmt.* 2 (Oct. 1992/93): 62-66.

The composer discusses his own choral work *Lauda alla poverta*. Includes musical examples.

B402. Lindholm, Steen. "Music in the Faroes." *Musical Denmark.* 43 (1990): 2-7.

Incomplete summary of the musical developments and organizations in the Faroes. Does not include list of composers or works.

B403. Lindholm, Steen. "Danish Choral Music Since 1900." *Nordic Sounds.* 3 (1995): 15-19.

Brief but informative sketch of the important choral composers, works, and choirs in this century.

B404. Lorentzen, Bent. "Myter i den nya musiken." *Nutida Musik.* 3 (1972/73): 55-56.

The composer discusses his own opera *Eurydike* (1965).

B405. Madsen, Flemming. "Crossing the Borders. New Goals for The Danish Music Information Centre." *Nordic Sounds.* 2 (1994): 23. Discusses current efforts by MIC to reach a broader international audience.

B406. Maegaard, Jan. "Metamorfose og variation." *dmt.* 3 (1952): 112.

The composer/theorist discusses the concept of "metamorphosis" - the most important and influential theory in the first half of the century in Danish contemporary music. He cautions against the overuse (and misuse) of the term, and asks whether in many cases what is called metamorphosis technique may in fact be simply thematic variation.

B407. Magnussen, Musse. "Kvinder komponerer, dirigerer og musikerer." *dmt.* 2 (1988/89): 71-72.

A brief survey of women composers, conductors and performers in Denmark, focusing on Nordens Kvindelige Symfoniorkester (The Nordic Women's Symphony Orchestra).

B408. Markow, R. "Soundprobe: Music from the Nordic Countries." *Music Magazine.* 12.2 (1989): 49-53.

B409. McCredie, Andrew. "Twentieth Century Danish Music." *Canon.* 13, 7/8 (March/April, 1960): 212-16.

B410. McCredie, Andrew. "Vagn Holmboe - a Versatile Nestor of Contemporary Danish Music." *The Chesterian.* 36, no.208 (Autumn 1961): 34-41.

B411. Mellnäs, Arne. "Vagn Holmboe - kvartettmästare." *Nutida Musik.* 5 (1962/63): 77-80.

Short overview of Holmboe as a string quartet composer. Brief analysis of his fourth quartet. Musical examples.

B412. Michelsen, Morten. "Unge danske: Svend Hvidtfelt Nielsen: nogle brikker til en mosaik." *dmt.* 3 (Nov. 1992/93): 85-91.

Portrait of composer Svend Hvidtfelt Nielsen. Includes list of works.

B413. Möldrup, Erling. "Guitar Music in Denmark from its Orgins to the Present Day." *Soundboard.* 13.3 (April 1987): 174+.

B414. Möldrup, Erling. "Third Danish Guitar Festival." *Classical Guitar.* 11: 9 (May 1993): 18-21.

B415. Mortensen, Tage. "Portræt af Jens Bjerre." *dmt.* 1 (1985/86): 12-15.

Profile of the composer. Complete work list.

B416. Munck, Tina. "MIC - Dansk Musik Informations Center: an important project in Danish musical life." *Musical Denmark.* 31 (1979/80): 2-4.

B417. *Musiken i Norden. Nordisk Tidsskrift för vetenskap, konst och industri.* 71: 1 (1995): 1+.

Special theme issue of *Nordisk Tidsskrift* on Scandinavian music. Several interesting articles pertaining to Danish music, including an informative article on Rued Langgaard (*see* B486).

B418. *MusikTexte.* 50 (Aug. 1993): 1+.

Special theme issue on Per Nørgård and his music. Includes articles by Per Nørgård, Karl Aage Rasmussen and Anders Beyer (analysis

of Nørgård's violin concerto *Helle Nacht*). Interview with the
composer by Erik Christensen. In German.

B419. Myers, Margaret. "Kvinnan som skapande musiker." *Musikrevy.* 1
(1988): 2-15.

A detailed discussion of the role of women in the music of
Scandinavia. A section on contemporary Danish women composers.

B420. Nielsen, Anne Kirstine. "Über weibliche Komponisten in
Skandinavien." *Neuland Ansätze zur Musik der Gegenwart.* 4
(1983/84): 128-32.

Survey of women composers in Scandinavia.

B421. Nielsen, Frede. "Some Danish Composers from 1600 to the
1960's." *dmt.* Special Issue in English (1971): 119-24.

Brief biographical sketches of thirty-four Danish composers, twenty-
five of whom are active in the 20th century. Selective work lists.

B422. Nielsen, Hanne Smith. "Musikkens åndedrag." *dmt.* 7 (May
1992/93): 224-25.

Portrait of composer Niels la Cour.

B423. Nielsen, Poul. "Der står en hjort ved en skovsø - om Ib Nørholms
musik." *Tá.* 1 (1967): 168.

B424. Nielsen, Poul. "Some comments on Vagn Holmboe's idea of
metamorphosis." *Dansk Årbog for Musikforskning.* VI (1968-72):
159-69.

B425. Nielsen, Svend Hvidtfelt. "*Windshapes* - et skoleeksempel." *dmt.* 7
(May 1992/93): 229-36.

Detailed analysis with many musical examples of Niels Rosing-
Schow's *Windshapes*.

B426. Nielsen, Tage. "Danish Music after Carl Nielsen." *Music Journal.*
21:3 (March 1963): 40-74 passim.

Informative overview of the prominent composers and their most important works in the three decades following Nielsen's death. An emphasis on symphonic works.

B427. Norden, Hugo. "Per Nørgård's *Canon.*" *The Fibonacci Quarterly.* 14, 2 (April 1976): 126-28.

Brief but technical analysis of *Canon* for organ, focusing on the use of the Fibonacci series in the work. Musical examples.

B428. *Nutida musik.* 5 (1962/63): 1+.

Special theme issue on Danish music. Several informative articles, portraits of important Danish composers, reviews of Danish musical life and activities, selective work lists, photos, musical examples.

B429. Nørgaard, Helmer. "The good old boys." *Musical Denmark.* 41 (1989): 10-14.

A look at the most prominent Danish composers of the generation following Carl Nielsen, including Vagn Holmboe, Knudåge Riisager, Herman D. Koppel, Svend Erik Tarp and Niels Viggo Bentzon.

B430. Nørgaard, Helmer. "Mens vi venter - Per Nørgård's debut." *Nutida Musik.* 2 (1956): 43-45.

Review of Per Nørgård's official debut. Provides an interesting insight into how the then 23 year old composer was viewed.

B431. Nørgaard, Helmer. "Vagn Holmboe-Nordboen." *Nordisk Musikkultur.* (1953): 50-53.

B432. Nørgård, Per. "Bevisthedsudvidelse ved fuld bevisthed." *Nutida Musik.* 4 (1972/73): 18-22.

Technical but somewhat abstract and esoteric discussion of the composer's infinity row theories and use of the Golden Mean (Fibonacci Series). Charts and examples.

B433. Nørgård, Per. "Drømmen at blive voksen - et monologisk fragment." *Nutida Musik.* 5 (1962/63): 14-17.

The composer discusses the search for one's style and musical voice as one "matures," and specifically breaks away from the Nordic tradition. Also discusses his work *Tre nocturner* (1961/62) for soprano and 19 instruments. One musical example.

B434. Nørgård, Per. "Hierarchic Genesis; Steps Towards a Natural Musical Theory." *Dansk Aarbog for Musikforskning.* 14 (1983). 70-75.

English translation of Per Nørgård's essay *Hierarkisk genesis: trin henimod en naturlig musikteori? Musikopleven som interferens mellem forventning og realisering (see* B107), in which his hierachic and infinity row theoretical concepts are explained in detail.

B435. Nørgård, Per. "The Idea Behind the Creation of Danish Radio's Television Interval Signal." *Numus West.* 1.4 (1973): 42-44.

The composer discusses the development of the "Interval Signal," a project to provide electronic music interludes for pauses between radio and television programs.

B436. Nørgård, Per. "Inside a Symphony." *Numus West.* 8 (Spring 1975): 4-16.

Detailed explanation of the infinity row theory with its melodic, rhythmic and harmonic aspects in the context of the composition of his *Third Symphony.* Charts and musical examples.

B437. Nørgård, Per. "Nya verk trivs bäst under motstånd." *Nutida Musik.* 3 (1971/72): 16.

Discusses the relationship between contemporary opera and traditional opera venues.

B438. Nørgård, Per. "Om *Experiment.*" *dmt.* 5/6 (1987/88): 190-1.

The composer discusses his own composition.

B439. Nørgård, Per. "Samarbejde - samfølelse." *Nutida Musik.* 3 (1956): 65-66.

Upon returning from the Nordic Music Days conference in Helsinki, the composer (then 23 years old and having only recently made his compositional debut. *See* B430.) laments the lack of interaction and unification of composers from the Scandinavian countries. The article caused quite a contraversy and prompted responses from several Nordic composers. *See also* B313 *and* B442.

B440. Nørgård, Per. "Statement zum Thema." *Neue Zeitschrift für Musik.* 6 (Nov. 1994): 30.

Per Nørgård and several prominent European composers discuss the topic "Schöne vs. Häßliche" ("Beauty vs. Ugliness").

B441. Nørgård, Per. "Striving for unique expression." *Finnish Music Quarterly.* 1 (1991): 47-49.

B442. Nørgård, Per. "Universal eller tidsbundet?" *Nutida Musik.* 2 (1957): 39-40.

Response to criticism received following the debate concerning the "universe of the Nordic mind" and cooperation between Nordic composers. *See also* B313 *and* B439.

B443. Nørgård, Per. "Worum dreht sich die Sache?" *MusikTexte.* 50 (Aug. 1993).

B444. Olsen, Ursula Andkjær. "At redigere det modern." *dmt.* 7 (May/June 1993/94): 240-41.

Commentary on Per Nørgård's 5th symphony.

B445. "Om Leif Kayser." *Norsk Musikkliv.* 4 (1942).

B446. Pade, Steen. "Antifoni - en analyse." *dmt.* 5 (March 1980): 221-228.

Part one of a two part analysis of Pelle Gudmundsen-Holmgreen's *Symfoni - Antifoni*, winner of the Nordic Council grand prize in 1980. Includes numerous musical examples and excerpts. *See also* B448.

B447. Pade, Steen. "Carl Nielsen and contemporary Danish music." *Nordic Sounds.* (1990): 5-7.

B448. Pade, Steen. "Symfoni - en analyse." *dmt.* 5 (March 1980): 229-231.

Part two of an analysis of Pelle Gudmundsen-Holmgreen's *Symfoni - Antifoni. See also* B446.

B449. Petersen, Frede Schandorf. "Vagn Holmboes femte symfoni." *Musikvärlden.* (1947): 270-72.

B450. "Program för Nordiska Musikdagarna i Stockholm, 8/9 - 11/9, 1960." *Nutida Musik.* 1 (1960/61): 25-67.

Includes concerts program, as well as brief bios, photos, and selective work lists for all the composers performed as part of the Nordic Music Days. Danish composers include Niels Viggo Bentzon, Gunnar Berg, Jan Maegaard, Tage Nielsen, Per Nørgård, and Flemming Weis.

B451. Rasmussen, Karl Aage. "Fuga i to tempi og tre satser." *dmt.* 1 (1982/83): 4-25.

Very interesting and informative interview with Per Nørgård and Pelle Gudmundsen-Holmgreen. Photos.

B452. Rasmussen, Karl Aage. "Ein Spiegel in einem Spiegel. Per Nørgårds Entdeckungsreise der Ohren." *MusikTexte.* 50 (Aug. 1993).

B453. Rasmussen, Per Erland. "Højt at flyve, vidt at skue: Forsøg på signalement af Mogens Winkel Holm." *dmt.* 2 (Oct. 1991/92): 38-44.

Portrait of the composer with musical examples. No list of works.

B454. Rasmussen, Per Erland. "Karsten Fundal - ung dansk komponist." *dmt.* 7 (May 1991/92): 229-235.

Portrait of composer Karsten Fundal. Includes musical examples and list of works.

B455. Rasmussen, Pia. "Women in Music: Seen from a Danish Perspective." *Fontes Artis Musicae.* 42/1 (Jan.-March, 1995): 26-34.

General overview of the contributions of women to Danish musical life. Brief description and history of important women composers, organizations and research centers. Bibliography.

B456. Ravnkilde, Svend and Bendt Viinholt Nielsen. "Rued Langgaards *Humoreske*: et postmodernistisk præ-ekko?!" *dmt.* 2 (1985/86): 69-73.

Analysis of *Humoreske*. Musical examples.

B457. Reel, James. "From Beginning to End: Danish Music on dacapo." *Fanfare*. 18:1 (Sept./Oct. 1994): 66-73.

Description of the Danish label dacapo, with a brief historical background, focus of the label and survey of major releases.

B458. Rosing-Schow, Niels. "Uden for båsene." *dmt*. 3 (1986/87): 124-137.

Portrait of composer Andy Pape. Includes musical examples and list of works.

B459. Rovsing Olsen, Poul. "Debussy og de nordiske lande." *Nutida Musik*. 5 (1962/63): 54-58.

Interesting article on the influence of Debussy and continental music in general on composers in Denmark and Scandinavia.

B460. Sandner, Wolfgang. "Thoughts on Germany and Nordic Music." *Nordic Sounds*. 2 (1994): 7-9.

A brief discussion of Scandinavian music from a German perspective.

B461. Savery, Uffe. "En drøm gik i opfyldelse." *Tværstand*. 26 (1996).

Discusses the appointment of the Safri Duo as the new official state music ensemble.

B462. Schiørring, Nils. "Musik og musikliv i Danmark omkring 1940." *Danmarks Kultur ved Aar 1940*. VIII (1943): 97-121.

B463. Schiørring, Nils. "Vagn Holmboe- a Danish composer." *Musical Denmark*. 5 (June 1954): 1-2.

B464. Schrøder, Regitze. "Al god dansk musik skal være tilgængelig." *KODAnyt*. 2 (1996).

Discussion of dacapo, the national music label.

B465. Schrøder, Regitze. "Han hører med øjnene og ser med ørerne." *KODAnyt*. 2 (1996).

Portrait of the composer and pianist Ilja Bergh.

B466. Schousboe, Torben. "Dänische musikwissenschaftliche Publikationen seit 1958." *Acta musicologica.* 44 (1972): 1-11.

An overview of musicological research centers, publishers, and authors of scholarly publication. Important works are summarized and organized by type and topic.

B467. Siegel, Wayne. "Electroacoustic Music in Denmark." *New World Music.* (Summer, 1996):

Survey of the development of electronic and computer music in Denmark, with a focus on DIEM (The Danish Institute of Electro-acoustic Music), which opened in 1986.

B468. Siegel, Wayne. "Live Electronics in Denmark: *Netværk*, an Experiment in Live Composition." *Contemporary Music Review.* 6:1 (1991): 205-17.

Discussion of the technical aspects (both hardware and software) and general analysis of *Netværk*, a collaborative real-time computer/MIDI composition by Siegel, Ivar Frounberg and Svend Aaquist Johansen. Charts and musical examples. Brief bios of the composers.

B469. Siegel, Wayne. "Nye tider for tonekunst." *Tværstand.* 27. (1996).

Discusses the changes made in the method of selection and distribution of funds for composers by Statens Kunstfond.

B470. Sjøgren, H. "Den nya musiken kommer fraan Esbjerg." *Tonfallet.* 5 (1990): 18-19.

B471. Sjøen, Gertie. "Choirs and orchestras collaborate on *Hexæmeron*, a new Danish work." *Nordic Sounds.* (March 1985): 13-14.

B472. Sjøen, Gertie. "Norwegian Contrasts and Danish Nuances." *Nordic Sounds.* (Sept. 1989): 15-17.

Interview with the Norwegian composer Knut Nystedt and the Danish composer Svend S. Schultz.

B473. Steensen, Steen Christian. "A decade of modern Danish opera." *Nordic Sounds.* 1 (1992): 10-11.

B474. Steensen, Steen Christian. "Upsurge in Danish Opera." *Musical Denmark.* (1992): 6-8.

B475. Storm, Staffan. "Minnewater - en introduktion." *Nudtida Musik.* 3 (1994).

An overview of Bent Sørensen's work *Minnewater,* performed at the 1994 ISCM Festival. In Norwegian.

B476. Sulc, M. "Aarhus festuge." *Hudebni Rozhledy.* 34 (1981): 548-49.

Review of the Aarhus Music Festival. In Czech.

B477. Sulc, M. "Aarhus festuge." *Hudebni Rozhledy.* 39 (1986): 18-19.

Review of the Aarhus Music Festival. In Czech.

B478. Thomas, Gavin. "Something Amiss with the Fairies." *The Musical Times.* 1815 (May 1994): 267-72.

Excellent article on Hans Abrahamsen, with interesting and insightful discussion of several works, including *Winternacht, Märchenbilder,* and *Nacht und Trompeten.* Musical examples.

B479. Thybo, Leif. "At være eller ikke være - Spredte bemærkninger vedrørende orgelkomponistens fortsatte eksistensberettigelse." *Nordisk Musikkultur.* (1952): 185-87.

B480. Thybo, Leif. "Ett utvecklingsdrag i Niels Viggo Bentzons musik." *Musikvärlden.* (1947): 139-42.

B481. Toncitch, V. "Impressions sur impressionnisme." *Anuario Musical; Revista de Musicologia del Consejo Superior de Investigaciones Cientificas.* 36 (1981): 157.

B482. Viinholt Nielsen, Bendt. "An Ecstatic Outsider: Rued Langgaard, 1893-1952." Transl. Anna Hedrick Harwell. *Fontes Artis Musicæ.* 42/1 (Jan.-March 1995): 36-50.

Excellent introduction and overview of the composer, his biography and music. Discussion of problematic issues pertaining to compiling a comprehensive Langgaard catalogue. Selected bibliography and discography.

B483. Viinholt Nielsen, Bendt. "Danish Music from the 1950's till Today." *Fontes Artis Musicæ.* 31 (March 1984): 176-82.

B484. Viinholt Nielsen, Bendt. "Om Rued Langgaard og kirkemusikken." Copenhagen: 1996. 3 p.

Discussion of Langgaard's role as a "church music" composer, and his beliefs pertaining to religion and art. First published as an article in *Skovshoved Avis,* 37 (Nov. 1993): 4. Revised in 1996 and published on-line (*see* R91).

B485. Viinholt Nielsen, Bendt. "Religion er en privatsag." *dmt.* 6 (May 1980): 295-97.

Background and history of Langgaard's opera *Antikrist.*

B486. Viinholt Nielsen, Bendt. "Rued Langgaard - en myte i nyt lys." *Nordisk Tidsskrift för vetenskap, konst och industri.* 71: 1 (1995).

In special theme issue *Musiken i Norden.* Good overview of Langgaard's life, place in Danish musical life, four production phases, and important works. Of value to both those new to Langgaard as well as those already familiar with his life and work.

B487. Viinholt Nielsen, Bendt. "Pettersson & Langgaard." *Nordic Sounds.* March 1988: 2-5.

B488. Wallner, Bo. "Om Rued Langgaard og *Sfærerenes Musik.*" *dmt.* 7-8 (1968): 174-79.

B489. Wallner, Bo. "Tonsättare och forskare." *Nutida Musik.* 5 (1962/63): 52-53.

Interview with Jan Maegaard.

B490. Wallner, Bo. "Vägar till nuet." *Nutida Musik.* 5 (1962/63): 2-8.

Excellent overview of the musical developments, debates and theories of composers in the first half of the century. Includes numerous quotes and excerpts from writings of various composers.

B491. Warnaby, John. "In relativ gesicherten Verhältnissen." *MusikTexte.* 56 (Nov. 1994): 50-51.

Discussion of 1994 Nordic Music Festival in Copenhagen. Brief reviews of particular works.

B492.   Warnaby, John. "A Meeting with Ib Nørholm." *Nordic Sounds.* 2 (1994): 10-13.

Interview with the composer while he was in residence at the 1993 Dartington International Summer School in England. Selective discography.

B493.   Wern, Vibeke. "Fra bruttoton til tonekunst." *dmt.* 7 (May 1992/93): 240-43.

Portrait of composer Hans-Henrik Nordstrøm.

B494.   Werner, Sven Erik. "DaCapo." *Nordic Sounds.* 2 (1992): 17-18.

Brief summary of the founding, mission, and activities of the dacapo record label.

B495.   Werner, Sven Erik. "Danish Musical Drama: a Miserable Success." *Musical Denmark.* 46 (1992):3-5.

B496.   Werner, Sven Erik. "*Qarrtsiluni* - The Sounding Silence." *Musical Denmark.* 53 (Dec. 1996): 4-7.

B497.   Wivel, Jakob. "An Other Opera." *Nordic Sounds.* 2 (1996): 8-11.

Review of the first two years of Den Anden Opera.

B498.   Würgler, Arne. "Et lille land i Europa: Kan Danmark overleve?" *Norsk Musikerblad.* 77.11 (1990): 4-6.

B499.   Zacharias, Walter. "Høffdings *Sinfonia concertante.*" *Levende Musik.* (1944): 29-33.

RESEARCH DIRECTORY

All addresses are in Denmark unless otherwise indicated.

Information Services
and Research Facilities

R1.   The Center for the Study of Danish Music.
       The University of Louisville, School of Music
       Louisville, KY 40292
       U.S.A.
       Tel: 502-852-5659 or 852-0540
       Fax: 502-852-0520
       e-mail: jmchri01@ulkyvm.louisville.edu
       Prof. Jean Christensen, Director

       Opened in 1996, it is the first research facility in the United States
       dedicated entirely to the study of Danish music.

R2.   Faroe Islands Music Information Centre.
       Reynagøta 12
       FR-100 Tórshavn
       Faroe Islands
       Tel: +298-14815
       Fax: +298-14825
       e-mail: summar@olivant.fo

R3.   Det Danske Kulturinstitut (The Danish Cultural Institute).
       Kultorvet 2
       1175 Copenhagen K
       Tel: +45 33 13 54 48
       Fax: +45 33 15 10 91

email:d-k-i@inet.uni-c.dk
Finn Andersen, Secretary General

R4.   Japan Scandinavia Music Centre.
       Yamato-higashi
       Yamato-shi Kanagawa
       Japan
       Tel/fax: +81 462 62 5610
       e-mail: aysn@yk.rim.or.jp
       Akiyoshi Nakamura, director

R5.   Kvinder i Musik (Women in Music).
       c/o Det Kgl Danske Musikkonservatorium
       Niels Brocks Gade 1
       1574 Copenhagen V
       Tel: +45 33 12 42 74
       Fax: +45 33 14 03 11
       Tove Krag, Head of Secretariat

       Publishes *Kvinder i Musik* (*see* B231). Research facility and archive
       open to the public.

R6.   MIC - Dansk Musik Informations Center (Danish Music Information
       Centre).
       Gråbrødre Torv 16
       1154 Copenhagen K
       Tel: +45 33 11 20 66
       Fax: +45 33 32 20 16
       e-mail: mic@mic.dk
       http://www.mic.dk
       Anette Faaborg, Director

       Center for the research, promotion, and archiving of Danish music,
       with a strong emphasis on music of the 20th century. Extensive
       collection and resources available for public use in addition to the
       knowledgeable staff make MIC an invaluabe research facility and
       source of information.

R7.   Nordic Music Archive.
       Ohio State University
       OSU Music/Dance Library
       Sullivant Hall
       N. High St.

Columbus, OH 43210
U.S.A.
Tel: 614-292-2319
Stephen Long, Director

Founded in 1988, the Nordic Music Archive has the largest
collection of music by Scandinavian composers in the United States,
with more than 1400 scores and 1000 recordings.

Music Organizations and Professional Associations

R8. AUT - Aarhus Unge Tonekunstnere.
Klostergade 52, 4. sal.
8000 Århus C
or: c/o Kasper Hemmer Pihl
Lille Elstedvej 271
8520 Lystrup
Tel: +45 86 74 13 50
e-mail: notabile@inet.uni-c.dk
Bo Gunge, Chairman

R9. DKF - Dansk Komponistforening (The Danish Composers Society).
Gråbrødretorv 16
1154 Copenhagen K
Tel: +45 33 13 54 05
Fax: +45 33 14 32 19
Mogens Winkel Holm, Chairman

R10. Dansk Kunstnerråd (Council of Danish Artists).
Amagertorv 13, 3.
1160 Copenhagen K
Tel: +45 33 32 82 92
Fax: +45 33 32 82 09
Kjeld Løfting, President

R11. Dansk Musikbiblioteks Forening (Danish Music Library Association)

Det Kgl. Bibliotek
Music Department
P.O.Box 2149
1016 Copenhagen K
Tel: +45 33 93 01 11

R12.   DMF - Dansk Musiker Forbund (Danish Musician's Union).
Skt. Hans Torv 26
2200 Copenhagen N
Tel: +45 35 24 02 40
Fax: +45 35 24 02 50
Anders Laursen, Chairman

R13.   DPA - Danske Poplærautorer (The Danish Songwriters Guild).
Gråbrødretorv 16, 1.
1154 Copenhagen K
Tel: +45 33 12 00 85
Fax: +45 33 91 02 85
Hans Dal, Chairman

R14.   Dansk Selskab for Musikforskning (Danish Musicological Society).
c/o Musikvidenskabeligt Institut ved Københavns Universitet
Klerkegade 2
1308 Copenhagen K
Tel: +45 33 11 27 26
Fax: +45 35 32 37 38
Niels Martin Jensen, Chairman

R15.   DUT - Det Unge Tonekunstnerselskab (The Society of Young
Composers).

Dismantled in 1994 due to internal, financial and political conflicts,
this important society was replaced by Musica Nova (*see* R23)

R16.   Felag Føroysk Tónaskald/Færørenes komponistforening (The
Society of Faroese Composers).
Postboks 324
Pæturssastova, Bringsnagøta
FR-100 Tórshavn
Faroe Islands
Tel:+298-1 3370
Pauli í Sandagerði, Foreman

R17. FUT - Fyns Unge Tonekunstnerselskab.
Det Fynske Musikkonservatorium
Islandsgade 2
5000 Odense C
Tel: +45 66 11 06 63
Fax: +45 66 17 77 63
Bertel Krarup, Chairman

R18. Fællesrådet for Udøvende Kunstnere (The Danish Council of
Performing Artists' Organizations).
Skt. Hans Torv 26
2200 Copenhagen N
Ejvind Callesen, Chairman

R19. Føroya Tónleikarafelag.
Pætursastova, Bringsnagøta
FR-100 Tórshavn
Faroe Islands
Tel: +298-1 3370

R20. Gruppen for Alternativ Musik (The Group for Alternative Music).

The Group for Alternative Music was formed in Copenhagen in
1972 by a group of young composers and performers to sponsor and
promote forms of new music outside of the "traditional" art-music
forms; i.e., performance art, multi-media, happenings, improvisatory
music, and avant-garde composition. Dissolved circa 1979.

R21. Koncertfelagið (Faroese Concert Society).
Hoydalsvegur 48
FR-100 Tórshavn
Faroe Islands
Tel:+298-1 8109
Bjarni Berg, Chairman

R22. Landsdelsorkestrenes Samråd (The Joint Council of the Regional
Symphony Orchestras).
Claus Bergs gade 9
Odense C
Tel: +45 66 12 00 57
Fax: +45 65 91 00 47

R23. Musica Nova.
Gråbrødre Torv 16, 2.
1154 Copenhagen K
Tel: +45 33 93 00 24
Fax: +45 33 93 00 24
e-mail: iscm-dk@inet.uni-c.dk
Lars Graugaard, Chairman

R24. NOMUS (the Nordic Music Committee).
Schönfeldts gränd 1
27 Stockholm
Sweden
Tel: 8 791 46 80/89
Fax: 8 21 34 68
Johan Falk, Secretary General

NOMUS is a subcommittee of the Nordic Council of Ministers,
dealing with the musical cooperation between the Scandinavian and
Baltic countries. Projects include commissions, conferences,
education, archiving, promotion, and publishing the NOMUS
Catalogue (*see* B173).

R25. NUT (Nordjyllands Unge Tonekunstnere).
Nordjysk Musikkonservatorium
Ryesgade 52
9000 Ålborg
Tel: +45 98 11 07 21
Fax: +45 98 11 37 63
Karl Petersen, Chairman

R26. Ny Musik i Birkerød.
c/o Kirsten Benn
Nørrevang 11
3460 Birkerød
Tel: +45 42 81 33 92
Kirsten Benn, Chairman

R27. SKRÆP, Eksperimental Musik Forum (Forum for Experimental
Music).
Kronprinsensgade 7
1114 Copenhagen K
Tel: +45 33 32 72 22

Fax: +45 33 32 72 34
Lone Arendal Winther, Director

R28.   Solistforeningen af 1921 (The Classical Soloist Association).
Vendersgade 24
1363 Copenhagen K
Tel: +45 33 33 06 51
Asger Lund Christiansen, President

Trade union for professional musicians in classical music.

Public Institutions

R29. Det Danske Kulturinstitut (The Danish Cultural Institute).
Kultorvet 2
Copenhagen K.
Tel: +45 33 13 54 48
Fax: +45 33 15 10 91

R30. Det kongelige Bibliotek - Musikafdelingen (The Royal Danish
Library - Music Department).
Box 2149
Copenhagen K
Tel: +45 33 93 01 11
Fax: +45 33 93 22 18
http://www.kb.dk/kb/geninfo/kbma.htm
Ebbe Lundgaard, Head of Department

The Music Department houses large collections of printed materials
and manuscripts by Danish composers as well as a collection of
orchestral and choral music for performances.

R31. Kulturministeriet (Ministry of Culture).
Nybrogade 2
P.O Box 2140
1015 Copenhagen K
Tel: +45 33 92 33 70
Fax: +45 33 91 33 88
e-mail: kum@kum.dk
http://www.kum.dk/
Jytte Hilden, Minister of Culture

R32. Statens Kunstfond (The State Arts Foundation).
      Sankt Annæ Plads 10B
      1250 Copenhagen K
      Tel: +45 33 11 36 01
      Fax: +45 33 11 35 06
      Vibeke Jakobsen, Head of Secretariat

      State-run foundation to support the arts through grants, commissions,
      subsidies, and awards to Danish artists.

R33. Landsbókasavnið (The Faroese National Library).
      J.C. Svabosgøta 16
      FR-100 Tórshavn
      Faroe Islands
      Tel: +298-1 1626

R34. Nordurlandahúsið i Føroyum/Nordens Hus (The Faroese Nordic
      House).
      Norðari Ringvegur
      FR-100 Tórshavn
      Faroe Islands
      Tel: +298-1 7900
      Fax: +298-1 9790
      Peter Turtschaninoff, Director

R35. Statens Musikråd (The Danish Music Council).
      Vesterbrogade 24
      1620 Copenhagen V
      Tel: +45 31 24 61 66
      Fax: +45 31 24 22 42
      Lennart Ricard, Chaiman.

      "Body of nine experts whose aim is the promotion of music life in
      Denmark. The council grants Dkr 150 million a year to musical
      activities with the Music Act as guidelines."[12]

R36. Statsbiblioteket, Statens Mediesamling (State and University
      Library/State Media Archive).
      c/o Statsbiblioteket
      Universitetsparken
      8000 Århus C
      Tel: +45 89 46 20 22

Fax: +45 89 46 20 50
Eva Fønss-Jørgensen, Head of Media Department

Teaching Institutions
and Conservatories

R37. Center for Rytmisk Musik og Bevegelse (The Centre for Improvised
Music and Movement).
Skoletorvet
Box 823
Silkeborg
Tel: +45 86 80 20 22
Fax: +45 86 80 24 66

R38. DIEM (Danish Institute of Electroacoustic Music).
Musikhuset Aarhus
Thomas Jensens Allé
8000 Århus C
Tel: +45 89 31 81 60
Fax: +45 89 31 80 66
e-mail: DIEM@daimi.aau.dk
http://www.daimi.aau.dk/~diem/
Wayne Siegel, Director

R39. Det Fynske Musikkonservatorium (The Carl Nielsen Academy of
Music).
Islandsgade 2
5000 Odense C
Tel: +45 66 11 06 63
Fax: +45 66 17 77 63
http://home1.inet.tele.dk/jbur/akons.htm

R40. Føroya Musikkskúli (The Faroese School of Music).
Falkavegur 6
FR-100 Tórshavn
Faroe Islands
Tel: +298-1 5555

R41. Institut for Musik og Musik terapi (Institute of Music and Music Therapy).
Aalborg Universitet
Kroghstræde 6
9220 Aalborg Ø
Tel: +45 98 15 85 22
Fax: +45 98 15 13 82
e-mail: martin@musik.auc.dk
http://www.musik.auc.dk/index.dk.html

R42. Institut for Musik og Musikvidenskab, Danmarks Lærerhøjskole (Music Dept., The Royal Danish School of Educational Studies).
Emdrupvej 54
Copenhagen NV
Tel: +45 39 69 66 33
Fax: +45 39 66 00 63

R43. Det Jyske Musikkonservatorium (The Royal Academy of Music, Århus).
Fuglesangsallé 26
8210 Århus V
Tel: +45 89 48 33 88
Fax: +45 89 48 33 22

R44. Det Kongelige Danske Musikkonservatorium (The Royal Danish Conservatory of Music).
Niels Brocks Gade 1
1574 Copenhagen V
Tel: +45 33 12 42 74
Fax: +45 33 14 09 11

R45. Musikvidenskabeligt Institut ved Aarhus Universitet (Musicology Department, Aarhus University).
Universitetsparken 220
8000 Århus C
Tel: +45 89 42 11 11

Fax: +45 86 42 31 29
http://www.aau.dk/dk/hum/musik/index.html

R46. Musikvidenskabeligt Institut ved Københavns Universitet
(Musicology Department, University of Copenhagen).
Klerkegade 2
1308 Copenhagen K
Tel: +45 35 32 37 39
Fax: +45 35 32 37 38
http://dorit.ihi.ku.dk/musik/index.html

R47. Nordjysk Musikkonservatorium (North Jutland Academy of Music).
Ryesgade 52
9000 Aalborg
Tel: +45 98 12 77 44
Fax: +45 98 11 37 63

R48. Operaakademiet (The Opera Academy).
Det Kongelige Teater
Postbox 2185
1017 Copenhagen K
Tel: +45 33 32 20 20
Fax: +45 33 14 46 06

R49. Rytmisk Musikkonservatorium (Rhythmic Music Conservatory).
Dr. Priemes Vej 3
1854 Frederiksberg C
Tel: +45 31 23 24 52
Fax: +45 31 22 07 56

R50. Vestjysk Musikkonservatorium (The West Jutland Conservatory of
Music).
Islandsgade 50
6700 Esbjerg
Tel: +45 76 10 43 00
Fax: +45 76 10 43 10
e-mail: vm@po.ia.dk
http://www.vm.dk/

Music Publishers

R51. Dansk Musikforlæggerforening (Danish Music Publishers'
    Association).
    P.O. Box 20
    6040 Egtved
    Tel: +45 75 55 14 11
    Fax: +45 75 55 23 16
    John Rasmussen, President

R52. Edition Egtved.
    P.O. Box 171
    Aaboulevarden 18
    8100 Aarhus C
    Tel: +45 86 20 20 70
    Fax: +45 86 12 00 44
    Ole Ugilt Jensen, Managing Director

R53. Edition Kontrapunkt.
    P.O. Box 35
    2930 Klampenborg
    Tel: +45 39 64 42 44
    Fax: +45 39 64 50 44
    Nils Winther, Managing Director

    In addition to publishing and printing music, Kontrapunkt is
    Denmark's largest classical music record label. Their primary focus
    in publishing printed music is the works of Ib Nørholm. *See also*
    R70.

R54.   Edition Wilhelm Hansen (WH).
       Bornholmgade 1, 1.
       1266 Copenhagen K
       Tel: +45 33 11 78 88
       Fax: +45 33 14 81 78
       e-mail: ewh@post1.tele.dk
       http://www.wilhelm-hansen.dk/
       http://www.freeworld.it/api/qualita/den.htm
       Tine Birger Christensen, Managing Director

       Largest publishing company in Denmark. The majority of
       prominent living Danish composers - as well as many of the
       important composers from the earlier part of the century - are
       published by WH.

R55.   EMI Music Publishing (Denmark) ApS.
       Mårkærvej 13
       2630 Tåstrup
       Tel: +45 43 71 19 30
       Fax: +45 43 71 19 45
       John Rasmussen, Managing Director

R56.   Engstrøm & Sødring.
       Borgergade 17
       1300 Copenhagen K
       Tel: +45 33 14 32 28
       Fax: +45 33 14 32 27
       Helge Schlenkert, Managing Director

R57.   Kleinerts Musik Forlag A/S & Mørks Musikforlag.
       Mårkærvej 13
       2630 Tåstrup
       Tel: +45 43 71 19 30
       Fax: +45 43 71 19 45
       John Rasmussen, Managing Director

R58.   SAMFUNDET (Samfundet til Udgivelse of Dansk Musik).
       Gråbrødrestræde 18, 1.
       1156 Copenhagen K
       Tel: +45 33 13 54 45
       Fax: +45 33 93 30 44
       e-mail: sudmusic@inet.uni-c.dk.
       http://www/samfundet.dk

Klaus Ib Jørgensen, President

Founded in 1871. Supported by the Danish Ministry of Culture with the purpose of publishing music by Danish composers.

R59. Warner/Chappell Music Denmark, A/S.
Anker Heegaards Gade 2, st. t.v.
1572 Copenhagen V
Tel: +45 33 13 33 15
Fax: +45 33 13 33 30
Finn Olafsson, Managing Director

Record Labels

Record labels that either specialize in or regularly release recordings
of classical and contemporary Danish music. All labels are located
in Denmark unless otherwise indicated.

R60.   BIS.
       Väringavägen 6
       63 Djursholm
       Sweden
       Tel: 08 755 4100
       U.S. distributor: Qualiton Imports. 24-02 40th Ave., Long Island,
       NY 11101.

       Swedish label that fairly regularly releases recordings of
       contemporary Danish music.

R61.   BMG Ariola Denmark A/S.
       Overgaden neden Vandet 17, 2.
       1414 Copenhagen K
       Tel: +45 31 57 99 22
       Fax: +45 31 57 07 90
       Lars Toft, Managing Director

R62.   Bridge Records.
       200 Clinton Ave.
       New Rochelle, NY 10801
       U.S.A.
       Tel: (914) 654-9270
       Fax: (914) 636-1383
       e-mail: bridgerec@aol.com

American label with a focus on contemporary music, particularly by American and Danish composers.

R63. Concertante.
Box 125
Odder
Tel: +45 86 54 56 77
Fax: +45 86 54 56 99

R64. dacapo.
Christianshavns Torv 2, 3.
1410 Copenhagen K
Tel: +45 32 96 06 02
Fax: +45 32 96 26 02

dacapo was formed as a result of Musikloven (the State Music Law) passed in 1989, with a mission to promote the ongoing, independant production and distribution of Danish music. dacapo releases 12-15 CDs yearly, approximately half of which comprise contemporary Danish repertoire. U.S. distributor: Naxos. 1165 Marlcrest, Suites E & F, Cherry Hill, NJ 08003.

R65. Danacord.
Gernersgade 35
1319 Copenhagen K
Tel: +45 33 15 17 16
Fax: +45 33 12 15 14
U.S. distributor: VAI Audio. 158 Linwood Plaza, Suite 301, Fort Lee, NJ 07024-3790.

R66. Danica Records.
Jersie Strandvej 5
Box 49
2680 Solrød Strand
Subdivision of OH-Music ApS.

R67. Dansk Musik Antologi (The Danish Music Anthology).

Dansk Musik Antologi was a private organization that until 1988 worked with EMI, Polydor/Phonogram, and Deutsche Grammophon to release Danish musical recordings. In 1989 Dansk Musik Antologi was replaced by the state-run organization Statslige

Pladeselskab (The National Recording Society) and its affiliated label, dacapo (*see* R64).

R68. Danmarks Radio.
Radiohuset
Rosenhørns Allé 22
Frederiksberg C
Tel: +45 35 20 30 40
Fax: +45 35 20 61 20

Denmark's National Radio occasionally releases CDs - primarily of live concerts and/or broadcasts of contemporary Danish music.

R69. DMF's Plademærke DK.
Vendersgade 25
Copenhagen K
Tel: +45 33 13 46 61
Fax: +45 33 14 51 75

Record label operated by Dansk Musiker Forbund (The Danish Musicians Union).

R70. Exlibris Musik.
Klarebodeme 3
1001 Copenhagen K
Tel: +45 33 11 07 75
Fax: +45 33 11 66 75

R71. Kontrapunkt.
P.O. Box 35
2930 Klampenborg
Tel: +45 39 64 42 44
Fax: +45 39 64 50 44
Nils Winther, Managing Director

Denmark's largest classical music record company. Kontrapunkt focuses solely on Danish music falling under two catagories: 1) Danish performances of any music from any time period, and 2) performances *of* Danish music of any period (though they have released numerous recordings of contemporary music). Subdivision of SteepleChase Productions. U.S. distributor: Allegro Corporation. 12630 N.E. Marx St., Portland, OR 97230-1059.

R72.   MXP, Danish Music Export & Promotion.
Skovvej 49
5700 Svendborg
Tel: +45 62 20 12 00
Fax: +45 62 20 19 60
Mikael Højris, Consultant

The purpose of MXP is the promotion and export of Danish music
on an international basis. MXP records and releases an annual series
of CDs of Danish music, with some focus on contemporary music.

R73.   OH Musik ApS.
Jersie Strandvej 5
P.O. Box 49
2680 Solrød Strand
Tel: +45 53 14 66 44
Fax: +45 53 14 66 67
Ole Høglund, President

R74.   Olufsen Records/Classico.
Sankt Knudsvej 8
1903 Frederiksberg C
Tel: +45 31 23 45 40
Fax: +45 31 31 14 97

R75.   Paula Records.
Sønderkær 323
7190 Billund
Tel: +45 75 33 11 10
Fax: +45 75 33 24 14
U.S. distributor: Albany Music Distributors. P.O. Box 5011,
Albany, NY 12205.

R76.   Point Records.
Jersie Strandvej 5
P.O. Box 49
2680 Solrød Strand
Subdivision of OH-Musik ApS. U.S. distributor: Albany Music
Distributors. P.O. Box 5011, Albany, NY 12205.

R77.   Spoof Records.
Schleppegrellsgade 8, baghuset
8000 Århus C

Tel: +45 86 13 06 54
Fax: +45 86 13 18 58

R78. SteepleChase Productions ApS.
      Box 35
      2930 Klampenborg
      Tel: +45 31 64 42 44
      Fax: +45 31 64 50 44

R79. Tutl.
      Reynagøta 12
      FR-100 Tórshavn
      Faroe Islands
      Tel: +298 14 81 5
      Fax: +298 14 82 5
      Kristian Blak, Managing Director

Copyright and Performance Rights Organizations

R80. Gramex.
Reventlowsgade 8, 1.
1651 Copenhagen V
Tel: +45 31 23 99 00
Fax: +45 31 23 09 31

"Established by the performing artists and phonogram producers for the collection and administration of neighbouring rights. The national ISRC agency."[13]

R81. KODA (Selskabet til forvaltning af internationale kompositionsrettigheder).
Landemærket 23-25
1016 Copenhagen K
Tel: +45 33 30 63 00
Fax: +45 33 30 63 30
e-mail: info@koda.dk
http://www.koda.dk/

The Society for the Administration of International Composition Rights, owned by the Danish Composer's Society, Danish Songwriters' Guild, Danish Society of Jazz, Rock and Folk Composers and Danish Music Publishers' Association. Member of the Nordisk Union, Nordisk Copyright Bureau.

R82. Nordisk Copyright Bureau (NCB).
       Frederiksgade 17
       Box 3064
       1021 Copenhagen K
       Tel: +45 33 12 87 00
       Fax: +45 33 12 42 62
       http://www.koda.dk/116.htm

       "NCB administers the mechanical rights in cooperation with the
       performance rights societies in Denmark (KODA), Finland
       (TEOSTO), Iceland (STEF), Norway (TONO), and Sweden
       (STIM)."[14]

Radio

R83.   Danmarks Radio (Danish National Radio).
       Radiohuset
       Rosenhørns Allé 22
       1999 Frederiksberg C
       Tel: +45 35 20 30 40
       Fax: +45 35 20 61 22
       http://www.dr.dk/
       Mogens Andersen, Director for Contemporary Music.

R84.   P2musik.
       Radiohuset
       Rosenørns Allé 22
       1999 Frederiksberg C
       Tel: +45 35 20 30 40
       Fax: +45 35 20 61 20
       Steen Frederiksen , Head of Music

       P2musik broadcasts serious music (including jazz), arranges about
       150 concerts per year and produces about 25-30 CDs per year in
       cooperation with record companies.

R85.   Útvarp Føroya/Færöarnes Radio (The Faroese Radio).
       Norðari Ringvegur
       FR-100 Tórshavn
       Faroe Islands
       Tel: +298-1 6566

Internet

Given the phenomenally rapid rate of growth and constantly changing nature of the internet, it is simply impossible to provide an all-inclusive list at this time of every internet location (i.e., internet sites, World Wide Web sites, ftp sites, newsgroups, internet bulletin boards, e-mail addresses, etc.) that may pertain in some way to 20th century Danish music. In an effort, however, to provide a starting point for this powerful research tool, some important World Wide Web sites (i.e., "websites") are included.

Only websites for *established institutions* that have been running for some time and are directly related to the topic are listed. No personal or privately run homepages are included, as they are likely to change or be eliminated altogether in a brief time period and are thus unreliable. Please note that even these established sites are subject to change; if a website is no longer accurate, current web-addresses for all the below listed institutions can be obtained by contacting MIC or the institutions directly via traditional methods of correspondence.

R86. DIEM.
       http://www.daimi.aau.dk/~diem/

       Website for The Danish Institute of Electroacoustic Music. Includes soundfiles, composer and staff biographies, information on the facilities and recent productions, and links to related topics.

R87. Jubii.
       http://www.jubii.dk/

A Danish search-engine and link-site focusing on music and the arts. Predominantly pop music and culture, though some classical music and composer links.

R88.   KODA.
http://www.koda.dk/

Website for the Danish performing and copyright association The Society for the Administration of International Composition Rights. Includes information and background about KODA, articles, and information for members and presenters regarding copyright and royalty laws as well as payment procedures.

R89.   Det Kongelige Teater.
http://kgl-teater.dk/dkt/

Includes season program for concerts, operas, ballets and theater at The Royal Theater, performer and director bios, press reviews, history of the theater itself, and ticket information.

R90.   The Danish Ministry of Culture.
http://www.kum.dk/

Informative website on the history, purpose, and activites of The Ministry of Culture. Includes access to several publications and links to related sites.

R91.   Kulternet Danmark.
http://www.kulturnet.dk/

A Danish web link-site focusing on culture and the arts, sponsored by The Danish Ministry of Culture. The purpose of Kulternet is to "use modern information technology in order to give better information about and better access to the resources and services of Danish cultural institutions. The main strategy for the achievement of this goal is to digitize the resources and collections of Danish cultural institutions and provide access to them via the World Wide Web."[15] Also includes an excellent research site for Rued Langgaard, with many articles, a complete biography, comprehensive work list, and extensive bibliography and discography. (http://www.kulturnet.dk:80/homes/langgaard/)

R92. MIC (The Danish Music Information Centre).
      http://www.mic.dk/

      Excellent research website for The Danish Music Information
      Centre. Includes recent news, numerous composer biographies,
      access to databases, a fairly comprehensive list of addresses, links to
      related sites, a selection of recent articles from *Musical Denmark*,
      discographies, upcoming events, and soundfiles.

R93. Musikhuset Aarhus.
      http://www.musikhuset-aarhus.dk/

      Built in 1982, Musikhuset is the home for the Aarhus Symphony
      Orchestra, the Jyske Opera, DIEM, the NUMUS festival and the
      Aarhus Festival. The website includes links to several of the above,
      as well as articles, tickets and booking information.

R94. Nordiskt Index över Klassisk Musik.
      http://hem.passagen.se/jcb/normus.n.html

      A web search engine and link-site focusing on classical music in
      Scandinavia.

R95. P2musik.
      http://www.dr.dk/p2musik/p2musik.htm

      Includes articles, reviews, performer and ensemble bios, concert
      programs, and monthly program-guide for P2 on Danmarks Radio.

R96. The Royal Danish Library, Music Dept.
      http://www.kb.dk/kb/dept/nbo/ma/index-en.htm

      Includes searchable on-line catalogue of The Royal Danish Library
      and links to other databases.

R97. SAMFUNDET.
      http://inet.uni-c.dk/~sudmusic/

      Includes searchable database for the SAMFUNDET catalogue.

R98. Statsbiblioteket, Musiksamlingen.
      http://www.sb.aau.dk/Old/musiksam.htm

Orchestras and Opera Companies

R99.   Aalborg Symfoniorkester (The Aalborg Symphony Orchestra).
        Kjellerupsgade 14
        9000 Aalborg
        Tel: +45 98 13 19 55
        Fax: +45 98 13 03 78
        Finn Schumacher, Musical Director
        Owain Arwel Hughes, Principal Conductor

        Regional orchestra of North Jutland. 63 players

R100.   Aarhus Symfoniorkester (Aarhus Symphony Orchestra).
        Thomas Jensens Allé
        Århus C
        Tel: +45 89 31 82 80
        Fax: +45 86 12 74 66
        Eri Klas, Principal Conductor

        Regional orchestra of central Jutland. 68 players.

R101.   Den Anden Opera (The Other Opera)
        Kronprinsensgade 7
        1114 Copenhagen K
        Tel: +45 33 32 38 30
        Fax: +45 33 32 38 36
        Jesper Lützhøft, Director

        Founded in 1994, it is the first theater in Scandinavia to specialize in
        contemporary opera and musical drama.

R102. Collegium Musicum
c/o Toke Lund Christiansen
Skovbogårds Allé 5
2500 Valby
Tel: +45 36 30 03 31
Fax: +45 36 30 63 64
Toke Lund Christiansen, Chairman
Michael Schønwandt, Principal Conductor and Artistic Director

Chamber orchestra performing symphonic music from the classical
period through the 20th century.

R103. Danmarks Radiosymfoniorkester (Danish National Radio Symphony
Orchestra).
Rosenørns Allé 22
1999 Frederiksberg C
Tel: +45 35 20 30 40
Fax: +45 35 20 61 21
http://www.dr.dk/p2musik/ensemble/radiosym.htm
Per Erik Veng, General Manager and Artistic Director
Ulf Schirmer, Principal Conductor

98 players. Regularly programs works by 20th century Danish
composers.

R104. Føroya Symfoni og Kamarorkestur (Faroese Symphony and
Chamber Orchestra).
Fosságøta
Klaksvík
Faroe Islands

R105. Den Jyske Opera (The Danish National Opera).
c/o Musikhuset Aarhus
Thomas Jensens Allé 22
8000 Århus C
Tel: +45 89 31 82 60
Fax: +45 86 13 37 10
Troels Kold, Director

R106. Det Kongelige Kapel (The Royal Danish Orchestra).
Postbox 2185
Det Kongelige Teater
1017 Copenhagen K

Tel: +45 33 32 20 20
Fax: +45 33 14 46 06
Michael Christiansen, General Manager
Pavo Berglund, Principal Conductor

Founded in 1448, Det Kongelige Kapel is the oldest continuous
music ensemble in the world. Also performs with the Royal Danish
Opera.

R107. Det Kongelige Opera (The Royal Danish Opera).
Kgs. Nytorv
P.O. Box 2185
1017 Copenhagen K
Tel: +45 33 32 20 20
Fax: +45 33 14 46 06
http://kgl-teater.dk/dkt/
Michael Christiansen, General Manager

Founded in 1748. 15 to 18 different operas per season. Performs
with Det Kongelige Kapel.

R108. Meginfelag fyri føroysk Hornorkestur
Suðurstiíggjur 3
FR-160 Argir
Faroe Islands
Tel: +298-1 4672
Ove Olsen, Director

R109. Musikteatret Undergrunden (The Underground Opera).
Aakandevej 20
3500 Værløse
Tel: +45 44 47 49 44
Fax: +45 44 47 49 88
Niels Pihl, Manager, Artistic Director and Stage Director

Founded in 1977, with a focus on contemporary repertoire and
works for children.

R110. Nordjyllands Amt Symfoniorkester (North Jutland Symphony
Orchestra).
c/o Rolf Werner Christensen
Aggersundvej 21
9690 Aars

or: c/o Erik Sahl
Svinkløvvej 347
9690 Fjerritslev
http://www.alco.dk/naso/frmain.htm

R111.   Odense Symfoniorkester (Odense Symphony Orchestra).
Claus Bergsgade 9
5000 Odense C
Tel: +45 66 12 00 57
Fax: +45 65 91 00 47
Per Holst, Manager
Jan Wagner, Principal Conductor

Regional orchestra of Fyn (Funen). 68 players.

R112.   Radiounderholdningsorkestret (Danish Radio Concert Orchestra).
Danmarks Radio
Radiohuset
Rosenhørns Allé 22
1999 Frederiksberg C
Tel: +45 35 20 30 40
Fax: +45 35 20 61 22
http://www.dr.dk/p2musik/ensemble/undhold.htm
Bent-Erik Rasmussen, Director
Hannu Koivula, Principal Conductor

Focus is on popular, "light" repertoire, though occasionally performs
serious 19th and 20th century works. Approx. 40-65 players.

R113.   Randers Byorkester (The Randers Chamber Orchestra)
c/o Værket
Mariagervej 6
8900 Randers
Tel: +45 86 41 28 33
Fax: +45 86 41 24 14
David Riddell, Managing Director and Artistic Director

R114.   Sjællands Symfoni Orkester (The Copenhagen Philharmonic
Orchestra).
Ny Kongensgade 13
1472 Copenhagen K
Tel: +45 33 91 11 99
Fax: +45 33 14 90 34

Tomas Vitek, General Manager
Heinrich Schiff, Principal Conductor

Regional orchestra of Sjælland (Zealand). 73 players.

R115. Sønderjyllands Symfoniorkester (Symphony Orchestra of South Jutland).
Musikhuset
Skovvej 16
6400 Sønderborg
Tel: +45 74 42 61 61
Fax: +45 74 42 61 06
Leif Balthzersen, Manager

Regional orchestra of Sønderjylland (South Jutland). 63 players.

R116. Tivolis Symfoniorkester (Tivoli Symphony Orchestra).

The name of Sjællands Symfoni Orkester during the summer months when it is in residence at Tivoli Gardens (*see* R114).

R117. Vestjysk Symfoniorkester (Symphony Orchestra of Western Jutland).
Islandsgade 50
Esbjerg
Tel: +45 75 13 93 99
Fax: +45 75 13 93 99

Performing Ensembles

This list is comprised of chamber ensembles and choirs that either specialize in or regularly perform contemporary Danish music. Contact information on each ensemble can be obtained from MIC.

R118.   Ars Nova: chamber choir specializing in Renaissance and 20th century music.

R119.   Athelas ensemble: large chamber ensemble.

R120.   The Boreas Wind Quintet

R121.   Cantus Borealis: chamber choir specializing in contemporary Færoese music.

R122.   Den Danske Trio (The Danish Trio): vln, vc, piano.

R123.   Den Danske Blæseroktet: wind octet.

R124.   Ensemble Nord: fl, clar, guitar, vc, piano, perc.

R125.   Esbjerg Kammerensemble: mixed chamber ensemble.

R126.   Den Fynske Trio: clar, vc, piano.

R127.   Grupo Novo Horizonte: choir.

R128.   Det Jyske Ensemble: fl, ob, clar, bsn, hrn, piano.

R129.   Embedsmandsduoen (The Civil Servant Duo): bassoon and keyboards

R130.   Kontrakvartetten (The Kontra Quartet): string quartet.

R131. Lille MUKO: chamber choir.

R132. LINensemble: chamber orchestra.

R133. Mad Cows Sing: large chamber ensemble.

R134. Musica Ficta: chamber choir specializing in Renaissance and 20th century music. Founded and directed by composer Bo Holten

R135. New Jungle Orchestra: mixed chamber orchestra w/electric instruments. The Danish State Ensemble, 1993-1996.

R136. The NM Ensemble: mixed chamber ensemble.

R137. Ny Dansk Saxofonkvartet (New Danish Saxophone Quartet): saxophone quartet.

R138. Odense Percussion: percussion sextet.

R139. Safri Duo: percussion duo. The Danish State Ensemble, 1997-2000.

R140. Sokkelund Sangkor: chamber choir.

R141. Storstrøms Kammerensemble (The Danish Chamber Players): chamber ensemble.

R142. The Sound of Choice Ensemble: 2 perc, 2 sax, guitar.

R143. Trio TSIAJ: piano trio.

R144. Tritonus: chamber choir.

R145. Århus Sinfonietta: large chamber ensemble.

Music Festivals

This is a partial list of music festivals in Denmark, listing those which either focus entirely on or have a significant portion devoted to Danish contemporary music.

R146. Contemporary Music in Suså.
Tyvelsevejen 26
Glumsø
Tel: +45 53 64 81 02

R147. Copenhagen International Experimental Music Festival (CIEF).
c/o SKRÆP
Kronprinsensgade 7
1114 Copenhagen K
Tel: +45 33 32 72 22
Fax: +45 33 32 72 34

R148. Copenhagen Summer Festival.
c/o Tatjana Kandel
Wesselsgade 13, 4.
2200 Copenhagen N
Tel: +45 31 39 60 33
Jens-Christian Lorenzen, Chairman

R149. Danish Composers' Biennale.
c/o Dansk Komponist Forening
Gråbrødretorv 16, 1.
1154 Copenhagen K
Tel: +45 33 13 54 05

Fax: +45 33 14 32 19
Mogens Winkel Holm, Chairman

R150. Ebeltoft Festival.
c/o Bent Lorentzen
Søtoften 37
Gentofte
Tel: +45 31 65 76 01

R151. Lerchenborg Musikdage (Lerchenborg Music Days).
Lerchenborg Slot
Kalundborg
Tel: +45 53 51 05 00, +45 31 62 97 47
Fax: +45 31 62 67 95

R152. Musiana.
c/o Louisiana Art Museum
3050 Humlebæk
Tel: +45 42 19 07 19
Fax: +45 42 19 35 05
Lars Fenger, Manager

R153. Musikhøst (Music Harvest).
c/o FUT
Islandsgade 2
5000 Odense C
Tel: +45 66 11 06 63
Fax: +45 66 17 77 63
Bertel Krarup, Director
Per Erland Rasmussen, Managing Director

R154. NUMUS-Festivalen.
Musikhuset
Thomas Jensens Allé
8000 Århus C
Tel: +45 89 31 82 00
Fax: +45 86 19 43 86
http://www.musikhuset-aarhus.dk/numus.html
Karl Aage Rasmussen, Director

R155. Ny Musik i Suså (Contemporary Music in Suså).
Tyvelsevej 26
4171 Glumsø

Tel: +45 53 64 81 02
Fax: +45 53 64 84 60
Hans-Henrik Nordstrøm, Director

R156. Scandinavian Festival of Music.
Helligkorsgade 18
Kolding
Tel: +45 75 50 94 99
Fax: +45 75 50 64 05

R157. Summartónar (The Faroe Islands Festival of Classical and
Contemporary Music).
Reynagøtu 12
FR-100 Tórshavn
Faroe Islands
Tel: +298 14815
Fax: +298 14825
Kristian Blak, Director

R158. UNM (Ung Nordisk Musik), dansk afdeling.
c/o Jesper Kock
Cort Adalersgade 5, 1 th.
1053 Copenhagen K
Tel: +45 33 15 30 26

R159. Århus Festuge (The Aarhus Festival)
Officersbygningen
Vester Allé 3
8000 Århus C
Tel: +45 89 31 82 70
Fax: +45 86 19 13 36
e-mail: festugeinfo@aarhusfestuge.dk
http://www.aarhusfestuge.dk/
Lars Seeberg, Artistic director

Notes

[1] RILM Abstracts of Music Literature(CD-ROM), 1994.

[2] Guy A. Marco, ed. *Information on Music: A Handbook of Reference Sources in European Languages.* 3 vols. (Littleton: Libraries Unlimited, Inc., 1984), 3: 101.

[3] Ibid., 102.

[4] Ibid., 97.

[5] Ivan Hansen, ed. *Per Nørgård; artikler 1962-1982.* (Copenhagen: Ivan Hansen, 1982), 308.

[6] Marco, *Information*, 102.

[7] Ibid., 96.

[8] Ibid., 104.

[9] Ibid., 99.

[10] Ibid., 106.

[11] Ibid., 101.

[12] Kim Bonfils, Mikael Højris and Bendt Viinholt Nielsen, eds. *Music in Denmark - Key Directory '96.* (Copenhagen: MIC, 1995), 36.

[13] Ibid., 9.

[14] Ibid., 9.

[15] Excerpted from the website.

Appendix 1: Chronological List of Danish Composers

The following is a list of Danish composers active in this century listed chronologically by year of birth and alphabetically within each year. The thirty most important and/or influential composers are printed in bold type.

It is a difficult task when comparing composers from different time periods and vastly disparate styles to judge who is more "important" or "influential;" terms which in and of themselves are somewhat speculative. Nonetheless, such a list is beneficial - if not essential - to providing perspective and benchmarks when reviewing the course of Danish music in this century. Though a certain amount of subjectivity is unavoidable and one may argue for the inclusion/exclusion of certain composers, this list is nevertheless an accurate summation based on several determining criteria.

Classification was based on consideration of the following factors: 1) level of international recognition; 2) importance in development of a particular style or movement; 3) notable contribution to Danish repertoire; 4) important regional figure; 5) important figure within a "generation;" 6) significant pedagogical role; or 7) pioneer in a particular style or genre, regardless of widespread acceptance or popularity.

1. Lange-Müller, Peter Erasmus (1850-1926)
2. Laub, Thomas (1852-1927)
3. Glass, Louis (1864-1936)
4. **Nielsen, Carl (1865-1931)**
5. Tofft, Alfred (1865-1931)
6. Godske-Nielsen, Svend (1867-1935)
7. Henriques, Valdemar Fini (1867-1940)
8. Høeberg, Georg (1872-1950)
9. Børrensen, Hakon (1876-1954)
10. Emborg, J.L. (1876-1957)
11. Nielsen, Ludolf (1876-1939)
12. Aagaard, Thorvald (1877-1937)
13. Crome, Fritz (1879-1948)

14. Gade, Jacob (1879-1963)
15. Gram, Peder (1881-1956)
16. Sandby, Harman (1881-1965)
17. Lauridsen, Laurids (1882-1946)
18. Bangert, Emilius (1883-1962)
19. Ring, Oluf (1884-1946)
20. Harder, Knud (1885-1967)
21. Salomon, Siegfred (1885-1962)
22. Grøndahl, Launy (1886-1960)
23. Reesen, Emil (1887-1964)
24. Raasted, N.O. (1888-1966)
25. Schierbeck, Poul (1888-1949)
26. Senstius, Kai (1889-1966)
27. Simonsen, Rudolph (1889-1947)
28. Andersen, Johannes (1890-1980)
29. Jacobsen, Ejnar (ç.1890-1970)
30. **Jeppesen, Knud (1892-1974)**
31. **Langgaard, Rued Immanuel (1893-1952)**
32. Brene, Erling (1896-1980)
33. Hye-Knudsen, Johan (1896-1975)
34. Bentzon, Jørgen (1897-1951)
35. Moe, Benna (1897-1983)
36. **Riisager, Knudåge (1897-1974)**
37. Hamerik, Ebbe (1898-1951)
38. Weis, Fleming (1898-1981)
39. Agerby, Aksel (1899-1942)
40. Agersnap, Harald (1899-1980)
41. **Høffding, Finn (1899-1997)**
42. Sandberg Nielsen, Otto (1900-1944)
43. Roikjer, Kjell (b.1901)
44. Bjerre, Jens (1903-1986)
45. Møller, Svend-Ove (1903-1949)
46. Syberg, Franz (1904-1955)
47. Christensen, Bernhard (b.1906)
48. Viderø, Finn (1906-1987)
49. Mortensen, Otto (1907-1986)
50. Jensen, Walter G. (b.1908)
51. **Koppel, Herman D. (b.1908)**

52. Tarp, Svend Erik (1908-1994)
53. **Berg, Gunnar (1909-1989)**
54. **Holmboe, Vagn (1909-1996)**
55. Kristensen, Svend Møller (1909-1991)
56. Zacharias, Walter (1909-1986)
57. Hjelmborg, Bjørn (1911-1994)
58. Jørgensen, Erik (b.1912)
59. Sennels, Richard (b.1912)
60. **Jersild, Jørgen (b.1913)**
61. Schultz, Svend S. (b.1913)
62. Andersen, Eyvind (b.1914)
63. Tofte-Hansen, Poul (b.1914)
64. Hansen, Johannes (1915-1985)
65. Madsen, Axel (b.1915)
66. Asmussen, Svend (b.1916)
67. Hænning, Otto (b.1916)
68. Nørgaard, Johannes (b.1916)
69. Harder, Egil (b.1917)
70. Martens, Ib (1918-1979)
71. **Bentzon, Niels Viggo (b.1919)**
72. Kayser, Leif (b.1919)
73. Nørlit, Poul Richard (b.1919)
74. Wellejus, Henning (b.1919)
75. Sark, Ejnar Trærup (b.1921)
76. Green, Ole-Carsten (b.1922)
77. **Rovsing Olsen, Poul (1922-1982)**
78. Thybo, Leif (b.1922)
79. Westergaard, Svend (1922-1988)
80. Nørgaard, Helmer (b.1923)
81. **Borup-Jørgensen, Axel (b.1924)**
82. Forsman, John Väinö (b.1924)
83. **Pade, Else Marie (b.1924)**
84. Viktor, Knud (b.1924)
85. Knudsen, Thorkild (b.1925)
86. Holm, Peder (b.1926)
87. **Maegaard, Jan (b.1926)**
88. Bergh, Ilja (b.1927)
89. Lund Christiansen, Asger (b.1927)

90. **Lewkovitch, Bernhard (b.1927)**
91. Høgenhaven Jensen, Knud (1928-1987)
92. Prytz, Holger (b.1928)
93. Schmidt, Ole (b.1928)
94. Bjerno, Erling D. (b.1929)
95. Nielsen, Tage (b.1929)
96. Lund, Gudrun (b.1930)
97. Lylloff, Bent (b.1930)
98. Plaetner, Jørgen (b.1930)
99. Larsen, Svend (b.1931)
100. **Nørholm, Ib (b.1931)**
101. Astrup, Bendt (b.1932)
102. Christiansen, Henning (b.1932)
103. **Gudmundsen-Homgreen, Pelle (b.1932)**
104. Hay, Diana Pereira (b.1932)
105. Mortensen, Tage (b.1932)
106. **Nørgård, Per (b.1932)**
107. Savery, Finn (b.1933)
108. Trede, Yngve Jan (b.1933)
109. Lautrup-Larsen, Hans (b. 1934)
110. **Lorentzen, Bent (b.1935)**
111. Norby, Erik (b.1936)
112. Tchicai, John (b.1936)
113. **Holm, Mogens Winkel (b.1936)**
114. Nielsen, Svend (b.1937)
115. Werner, Sven Erik (b.1937)
116. Dahl, Vivian (b.1938)
117. Gislinge, Frederik (b.1938)
118. Kammerer, Edwin (b.1938)
119. **"Fuzzy" (Jens Wilhelm Pedersen) (b.1939)**
120. Høybye, John (b.1939)
121. Levy, Morten (b.1939)
122. Korsgaard, Bjarne (b.1941)
123. Larsen, Kurt (b.1941)
124. Martinussen, Leif (b.1941)
125. Mikkelborg, Palle (b.1941)
126. Alsted, Birgitte (b.1942)
127. Gabold, Ingolf (b.1942)
128. Tanggaard, Svend Erik (b.1942)

129. Andersen, Eric (b.1943)
130. Kongsted, Ole (b. 1943)
131. Mortensen, Jørgen (b.1943)
132. Møldrup, Erling (b.1943)
133. Møller Pedersen, Gunnar (b.1943)
134. Olsson, Birgitta Holst (b.1943)
135. Philip, Hans-Erik (b.1943)
136. Vogel, Karsten (b.1943)
137. Ørvad, Timme (b.1943)
138. Colding-Jørgensen, Henrik (b.1944)
139. Keller, Jens Christoffer (b.1944)
140. Koppel, Thomas (b.1944)
141. la Cour, Niels (b.1944)
142. Simonsen, Anker Fjeld (b.1944)
143. **Buck, Ole (b.1945)**
144. Hansen, Anthon (b.1945)
145. Hansen, Ole Kock (b.1945)
146. Kullberg, Erling (b.1945)
147. Stolarczyk, Willy (b.1945)
148. Ørvad, Hanne (b.1945)
149. Bach, Erik (b.1946)
150. Bitsch, Frode (b. 1946)
151. Dørge, Pierre (b.1946)
152. Hersbo, Bjarne (b.1946)
153. Knudsen, Kenneth (b.1946)
154. Malmgren, Jens-Ole (b.1946)
155. Petersen, Nils Holger (b.1946)
156. Bisgaard, Lars (b.1947)
157. Holbech, Bent Peder (b.1947)
158. Kengen, Knud-Erik (b.1947)
159. Koppel, Anders (b.1947)
160. Kühl, Karl Erik (b.1947)
161. Lacy, Butch (b.1947)
162. Lund Christiansen, Toke (b.1947)
163. Møller, Peter (b.1947)
164. Nordstrøm, Hans-Henrik (b.1947)
165. Norup, Helle Merete (b.1947)
166. **Rasmussen, Karl Aage (b.1947)**
167. Barfoed, Anders (b.1948)

168. Bech, John F. (b.1948)
169. **Holten, Bo (b.1948)**
170. Ikilikian, Arshak (b.1948)
171. Johansen, Svend Aaquist (b.1948)
172. Lekfeldt, Jørgen (b.1948)
173. Christensen, Jan (b.1949)
174. Fabricius, Jacob Christian (b. 1949)
175. Hansen, Lars Kristian (b.1949)
176. Nilsson, Lasse (b.1949)
177. **Ruders, Poul (b.1949)**
178. Rømer, Hanne (b.1949)
179. Barfoed, Søren (b.1950)
180. **Frounberg, Ivar (b.1950)**
181. Hegaard, Lars (b.1950)
182. Rasmussen, Niels Christian (b.1950)
183. Schultz, Lars Peter (b.1950)
184. Bergstrøm-Nielsen, Carl (b.1951)
185. Bach, Hans-Jørgen (Gutten) (b.1952)
186. Nielsen-Bergstrøm, Carl (b.1951)
187. **Abrahamsen, Hans (b.1952)**
188. Haumann, Erik (b.1952)
189. Johansen, Jens (b.1952)
190. Emborg, Jørgen (b.1953)
191. Linnet, Anne (b.1953)
192. Siegel, Wayne (b.1953)
193. Højsgaard, Erik (b.1954)
194. Jepsen, Henning (b.1954)
195. Rosing-Schow, Niels (b.1954)
196. Brødsgaard, Anders (b.1955)
197. Callesen, Jan Thor (b.1955)
198. **Christensen, Mogens (b.1955)**
199. Hendze, Jesper (b.1955)
200. Pape, Andy (b.1955)
201. Sjøgren, Kim (b.1955)
202. Borg, Matti (b.1956)
203. Dynnesen, Lise (b.1956)
204. Fievé, Peter (b.1956)
205. Fjeldmose, Lars (b.1956)

206. Frandsen, John (b.1956)
207. Helwig, Kim (b.1956)
208. Pade, Steen (b.1956)
209. Graugaard, Lars Henrik (b.1957)
210. **Sørensen, Bent (b.1958)**
211. Hvidtfelt Nielsen, Svend (b.1958)
212. Riishøjgaard, Knud (b.1959)
213. Engberg, Christina Wagner (b.1960)
214. Nordentoft, Anders (b.1960)
215. Friis, Flemming (b.1961)
216. Olsen, Morten (b.1961)
217. Hyldgaard, Søren (b.1962)
218. Andersen, Bo (b. 1963)
219. Marthinsen, Niels (b.1963)
220. Nyvang, Michael (b.1963)
221. Teglbjærg, Hans Peter Stubbe (b.1963)
222. Gunge, Bo (b.1964)
223. Henriksen, Stephen (b.1964)
224. Jæger, Bo Lundby (b.1964)
225. Kondrup, Eva Noer (b.1964)
226. Kanding, Ejnar (b.1965)
227. Klit, Lars (b.1965)
228. Åkerwall, Martin (b.1965)
229. Fundal, Karsten (b.1966)
230. Lester, Thomas (b.1966)
231. Jørgensen, Klaus Ib (b. 1967)
232. Koch, Jesper (b.1967)
233. Bruun, Peter (b.1968)
234. Hansen, Flemming Christian (b.1968)
235. Agerfeldt Olesen, Thomas (b.1969)
236. Hørsving, Jens (b.1969)
237. Laursen, Lasse (b.1969)
238. Palsmar, Martin (b.1970)
239. Christensen, Simon (b.1971)
240. Hodkinson, Juliana (b.1971)
241. Holmen, Jesper Henrik (b.1971)
242. Magle, Frederik (b.1977)

FAROESE COMPOSERS:

1. Waagstein, Joen (1879-1949)
2. Heinsesen, William (1900-1991)
3. **Blak, Kristian (b.1947)**
4. Bæk, Kári (b.1950)
5. Berg, Bjarni (b.1954)
6. Restorff, Bjarni (b.1955)
7. Sandagerði, Pauli í (b.1955)
8. Nyholm Debess, Edvard (b.1960)
9. Rasmussen, Sunleif (b.1961)
10. Meitil, Heðin (b.1963)
11. Petersen, Atli Kárason (b.1963)
12. Bogason, Tróndur (b. 1976)

Appendix 2: Alphabetical List of Danish Composers

1. Aagaard, Thorvald (1877-1937)
2. Abrahamsen, Hans (b.1952)
3. Agerby, Aksel (1899-1942)
4. Agerfeldt Olesen, Thomas (b.1969)
5. Agersnap, Harald (1899-1980)
6. Alsted, Birgitte (b.1942)
7. Andersen, Bo (b. 1963)
8. Andersen, Eric (b.1943)
9. Andersen, Eyvind (b.1914)
10. Andersen, Johannes (1890-1980)
11. Asmussen, Svend (b.1916)
12. Astrup, Bendt (b.1932)
13. Bach, Erik (b.1946)
14. Bach, Hans-Jørgen (Gutten) (b.1952)
15. Bangert, Emilius (1883-1962)
16. Barfoed, Anders (b.1948)
17. Barfoed, Søren (b.1950)
18. Bech, John F. (b.1948)
19. Bentzon, Jørgen (1897-1951)
20. Bentzon, Niels Viggo (b.1919)
21. Berg, Gunnar (1909-1989)
22. Bergh, Ilja (b.1927)
23. Bergstrøm-Nielsen, Carl (b.1951)
24. Bisgaard, Lars (b.1947)
25. Bitsch, Frode (b. 1946)
26. Bjerno, Erling D. (b.1929)
27. Bjerre, Jens (1903-1986)
28. Borg, Matti (b.1956)
29. Borup-Jørgensen, Axel (b.1924)
30. Brene, Erling (1896-1980)
31. Bruun, Peter (b.1968)
32. Brødsgaard, Anders (b.1955)
33. Buck, Ole (b.1945)
34. Børrensen, Hakon (1876-1954)
35. Callesen, Jan Thor (b.1955)
36. Christensen, Bernhard (b.1906)
37. Christensen, Jan (b.1949)
38. Christensen, Mogens (b.1955)
39. Christensen, Simon (b.1971)
40. Christiansen, Henning (b.1932)
41. Colding-Jørgensen, Henrik (b.1944)
42. Crome, Fritz (1879-1948)
43. Dahl, Vivian (b.1938)
44. Dynnesen, Lise (b.1956)
45. Dørge, Pierre (b.1946)
46. Emborg, J.L. (1876-1957)

47. Emborg, Jørgen (b.1953)
48. Engberg, Christina Wagner (b.1960)
49. Fabricius, Jacob Christian (b. 1949)
50. Fievé, Peter (b.1956)
51. Fjeldmose, Lars (b.1956)
52. Forsman, John Väinö (b.1924)
53. Frandsen, John (b.1956)
54. Friis, Flemming (b.1961)
55. Frounberg, Ivar (b.1950)
56. Fundal, Karsten (b.1966)
57. "Fuzzy" (Jens Wilhelm Pedersen) (b.1939)
58. Gabold, Ingolf (b.1942)
59. Gade, Jacob (1879-1963)
60. Gislinge, Frederik (b.1938)
61. Glass, Louis (1864-1936)
62. Godske-Nielsen, Svend (1867-1935)
63. Gram, Peder (1881-1956)
64. Graugaard, Lars Henrik (b.1957)
65. Green, Ole-Carsten (b.1922)
66. Grøndahl, Launy (1886-1960)
67. Gudmundsen-Homgreen, Pelle (b.1932)
68. Gunge, Bo (b.1964)
69. Hamerik, Ebbe (1898-1951)
70. Hansen, Anthon (b.1945)
71. Hansen, Flemming Christian (b.1968)
72. Hansen, Johannes (1915-1985)
73. Hansen, Lars Kristian (b.1949)
74. Hansen, Ole Kock (b.1945)
75. Harder, Egil (b.1917)
76. Harder, Knud (1885-1967)
77. Haumann, Erik (b.1952)
78. Hay, Diana Pereira (b.1932)
79. Hegaard, Lars (b.1950)
80. Helwig, Kim (b.1956)
81. Hendze, Jesper (b.1955)
82. Henriksen, Stephen (b.1964)
83. Henriques, Valdemar Fini (1867-1940)
84. Hersbo, Bjarne (b.1946)
85. Hjelmborg, Bjørn (1911-1994)
86. Hodkinson, Juliana (b.1971)
87. Holbech, Bent Peder (b.1947)
88. Holm, Mogens Winkel (b.1936)
89. Holm, Peder (b.1926)
90. Holmboe, Vagn (1909-1996)
91. Holmen, Jesper Henrik (b.1971)
92. Holten, Bo (b.1948)
93. Hvidtfelt Nielsen, Svend (b.1958)
94. Hye-Knudsen, Johan (1896-1975)
95. Hyldgaard, Søren (b.1962)
96. Hænning, Otto (b.1916)
97. Høeberg, Georg (1872-1950)
98. Høffding, Finn (1899-1997)
99. Høgenhaven Jensen, Knud (1928-1987)
100. Højsgaard, Erik (b.1954)
101. Hørsving, Jens (b.1969)
102. Høybye, John (b.1939)
103. Ikilikian, Arshak (b.1948)
104. Jacobsen, Ejnar (c.1890-1970)
105. Jensen, Walter G. (b.1908)
106. Jeppesen, Knud (1892-1974)
107. Jepsen, Henning (b.1954)
108. Jersild, Jørgen (b.1913)
109. Johansen, Jens (b.1952)
110. Johansen, Svend Aaquist (b.1948)
111. Jæger, Bo Lundby (b.1964)
112. Jørgensen, Erik (b.1912)
113. Jørgensen, Klaus Ib (b. 1967)
114. Kammerer, Edwin (b.1938)
115. Kanding, Ejnar (b.1965)
116. Kayser, Leif (b.1919)
117. Keller, Jens Christoffer (b.1944)
118. Kengen, Knud-Erik (b.1947)
119. Klit, Lars (b.1965)
120. Knudsen, Kenneth (b.1946)
121. Knudsen, Thorkild (b.1925)

122. Koch, Jesper (b.1967)
123. Kondrup, Eva Noer (b.1964)
124. Kongsted, Ole (b. 1943)
125. Koppel, Anders (b.1947)
126. Koppel, Herman D. (b.1908)
127. Koppel, Thomas (b.1944)
128. Korsgaard, Bjarne (b.1941)
129. Kristensen, Svend Møller (1909-1991)
130. Kühl, Karl Erik (b.1947)
131. Kullberg, Erling (b.1945)
132. la Cour, Niels (b.1944)
133. Lacy, Butch (b.1947)
134. Lange-Müller, Peter Erasmus (1850-1926)
135. Langgaard, Rued Immanuel (1893-1952)
136. Larsen, Kurt (b.1941)
137. Larsen, Svend (b.1931)
138. Laub, Thomas (1852-1927)
139. Lauridsen, Laurids (1882-1946)
140. Laursen, Lasse (b.1969)
141. Lautrup-Larsen, Hans (b. 1934)
142. Lekfeldt, Jørgen (b.1948)
143. Lester, Thomas (b.1966)
144. Levy, Morten (b.1939)
145. Lewkovitch, Bernhard (b.1927)
146. Linnet, Anne (b.1953)
147. Lorentzen, Bent (b.1935)
148. Lund Christiansen, Asger (b.1927)
149. Lund Christiansen, Toke (b.1947)
150. Lund, Gudrun (b.1930)
151. Lylloff, Bent (b.1930)
152. Madsen, Axel (b.1915)
153. Maegaard, Jan (b.1926)
154. Magle, Frederik (b.1977)
155. Malmgren, Jens-Ole (b.1946)
156. Martens, Ib (1918-1979)
157. Marthinsen, Niels (b.1963)
158. Martinussen, Leif (b.1941)
159. Mikkelborg, Palle (b.1941)
160. Moe, Benna (1897-1983)
161. Mortensen, Jørgen (b.1943)
162. Mortensen, Otto (1907-1986)
163. Mortensen, Tage (b.1932)
164. Møldrup, Erling (b.1943)
165. Møller Pedersen, Gunnar (b.1943)
166. Møller, Peter (b.1947)
167. Møller, Svend-Ove (1903-1949)
168. Nielsen, Carl (1865-1931)
169. Nielsen, Ludolf (1876-1939)
170. Nielsen, Svend (b.1937)
171. Nielsen, Tage (b.1929)
172. Nielsen-Bergstrøm, Carl (b.1951)
173. Nilsson, Lasse (b.1949)
174. Norby, Erik (b.1936)
175. Nordentoft, Anders (b.1960)
176. Nordstrøm, Hans-Henrik (b.1947)
177. Norup, Helle Merete (b.1947)
178. Nyvang, Michael (b.1963)
179. Nørgaard, Helmer (b.1923)
180. Nørgaard, Johannes (b.1916)
181. Nørgård, Per (b.1932)
182. Nørholm, Ib (b.1931)
183. Nørlit, Poul Richard (b.1919)
184. Olsen, Morten (b.1961)
185. Olsson, Birgitta Holst (b.1943)
186. Pade, Else Marie (b.1924)
187. Pade, Steen (b.1956)
188. Palsmar, Martin (b.1970)
189. Pape, Andy (b.1955)
190. Petersen, Nils Holger (b.1946)
191. Philip, Hans-Erik (b.1943)
192. Plaetner, Jørgen (b.1930)
193. Prytz, Holger (b.1928)
194. Raasted, N.O. (1888-1966)
195. Rasmussen, Karl Aage (b.1947)
196. Rasmussen, Niels Christian (b.1950)
197. Reesen, Emil (1887-1964)
198. Riisager, Knudåge (1897-1974)
199. Riishøjgaard, Knud (b.1959)
200. Ring, Oluf (1884-1946)

201. Roikjer, Kjell (b.1901)
202. Rosing-Schow, Niels (b.1954)
203. Rovsing Olsen, Poul (1922-1982)
204. Ruders, Poul (b.1949)
205. Rømer, Hanne (b.1949)
206. Salomon, Siegfred (1885-1962)
207. Sandberg Nielsen, Otto (1900-1944)
208. Sandby, Harman (1881-1965)
209. Sark, Ejnar Trærup (b.1921)
210. Savery, Finn (b.1933)
211. Schierbeck, Poul (1888-1949)
212. Schmidt, Ole (b.1928)
213. Schultz, Lars Peter (b.1950)
214. Schultz, Svend S. (b.1913)
215. Sennels, Richard (b.1912)
216. Senstius, Kai (1889-1966)
217. Siegel, Wayne (b.1953)
218. Simonsen, Anker Fjeld (b.1944)
219. Simonsen, Rudolph (1889-1947)
220. Sjøgren, Kim (b.1955)
221. Stolarczyk, Willy (b.1945)
222. Syberg, Franz (1904-1955)
223. Sørensen, Bent (b.1958)
224. Tanggaard, Svend Erik (b.1942)
225. Tarp, Svend Erik (1908-1994)
226. Tchicai, John (b.1936)
227. Teglbjærg, Hans Peter Stubbe (b.1963)
228. Thybo, Leif (b.1922)
229. Tofft, Alfred (1865-1931)
230. Tofte-Hansen, Poul (b.1914)

231. Trede, Yngve Jan (b.1933)
232. Viderø, Finn (1906-1987)
233. Viktor, Knud (b.1924)
234. Vogel, Karsten (b.1943)
235. Weis, Fleming (1898-1981)
236. Wellejus, Henning (b.1919)
237. Werner, Sven Erik (b.1937)
238. Westergaard, Svend (1922-1988)
239. Zacharias, Walter (1909-1986)
240. Ørvad, Hanne (b.1945)
241. Ørvad, Timme (b.1943)
242. Åkerwall, Martin (b.1965)

FAROESE COMPOSERS:

1. Berg, Bjarni (b.1954)
2. Blak, Kristian (b.1947)
3. Bogason, Tróndur (b. 1976)
4. Bæk, Kári (b.1950)
5. Heinsesen, William (1900-1991)
6. Meitil, Heðin (b.1963)
7. Nyholm Debess, Edvard (b.1960)
8. Petersen, Atli Kárason (b.1963)
9. Rasmussen, Sunleif (b.1961)
10. Restorff, Bjarni (b.1955)
11. Sandagerði, Pauli í (b.1955)
12. Waagstein, Joen (1879-1949)

Index

Numbers preceded by a "B" refer to the BIBLIOGRAPHY; numbers preceded by an "R" refer to the RESEARCH DIRECTORY. Subjects, titles and names of organizations are listed in English; formal names of persons and places are listed in the original language.

Only those composers, persons, and ensembles covered specifically in a cited source appear in the index; for a full list of composers refer to the appendices, for other names and items refer to the respective sections within the body of the work.

Specific works are listed by composer and appear last in the composer citation in alphabetical order. Note that only works which are the primary focus of a source appear in the index; the hundreds of other works mentioned in passing are not listed by title. For individual authors refer to the body of the work.

Works, complete, B162
Mascarade, B275
Qarrtsiluni, B254, B378
Ring, Oluf, B276
Rosing-Schow, Niels:
Dommen, B383
Windshapes, B425
Rovsing Olsen, Poul, B278,
B329, B365, B367, B426,
B459
Royal Danish Ballet, B20, B31,
B39, B40, B64, B65, B66,
B76, B178, B378, R89. *See
also* Ballet
Royal Danish Opera. *See* Opera
Royal Danish Theatre, B76, R89
Ruders, Poul, B26, B118, B119,
B256, B277
Concerto in Pieces, B4

Safri Duo, B461, R139
SAMFUNDET (Samfundet til
udgivelse af dansk musik),
B132, B178, B223, B369, R58,
R97
Sandby, Harman, B59, B348
Savery, Finn, B291, B310
Works of, B175
Schierbeck, Poul, B59, B85, B86,
B348
Schultz, Svend S., B2, B59, B60,
B114, B339, B344, B348,
B351, B426, B472
Senstius, Kai, B348
Siegel, Wayne, B467, B468,
B469. *See also* DIEM

Smitt, Christina Wagner. *See*
Engborg, Christina Wagner
Sub Rosa, B58, B298
Syberg, Franz, B379
Symphony orchestras, B1, B112,
B148, B407, R22. *See also*
ORCHESTRAS AND OPERA
COMPANIES *section*
Sæverud, Harald, B349
Sørensen, Bent, B264, B269
Minnewater, B475
Sørensen, Søren, B35, B83, B142

Tarp, Svend Erik, B349
Television. *See* Media
Thybo, Leif, B147, B267, B426,
B479, B480

Viderø, Finn, B348

Waagstein, Joen, B158
Weis, Flemming, B59, B60,
B114, B344, B365, B367,
B450, B490
Westergaard, Svend, B114, B351,
B426
Wilhelm Pedersen, Jens. *See*
"Fuzzy"
Williams, Margaret, B283
Winkel-Holm, Mogens. *See*
Holm, Mogens Winkel
Women composers/musicians in
Denmark, B77, B120, B231,
B282, B283, B284, B407,
B419, B420, B455, R5

Ørvad, Hanne, B284

About the Author

LANSING D. McLOSKEY is a Ph. D. candidate with the Harvard University Department of Music. He holds degrees in music composition from the University of Southern California School of Music and the University of California, Santa Barbara. A lecturer and recognized authority on Danish Music, he is the recipient of several national and international awards.